QuickCook

QuickCook
Italian

Joy Skipper

Every dish, three ways —you choose!
30 minutes | 20 minutes | 10 minutes

An Hachette UK Company
www.hachette.co.uk

First published in Great Britain in 2012 by Hamlyn,
a division of Octopus Publishing Group Ltd
Endeavour House, 189 Shaftesbury Avenue
London WC2H 8JY
www.octopusbooks.co.uk
www.octopusbooksusa.com

Distributed in the US by Hachette Book Group USA
237 Park Avenue, New York NY 10017 USA

Distributed in Canada by Canadian Manda Group
165 Dufferin Street, Toronto, Ontario, Canada M6K 3H6

ISBN 978-0-600-62512-4

Printed and bound in China

10 9 8 7 6 5 4 3 2 1

Standard level spoon and cup measurements are used in all recipes.

Ovens should be preheated to the specified temperature. If using a convection oven,
follow the manufacturer's instructions for adjusting the time and temperature.
Broilers should also be preheated.

This book includes dishes made with nuts and nut derivatives. It is advisable for
those with known allergic reactions to nuts and nut derivatives and those who may
be potentially vulnerable to these allergies, such as pregnant and nursing mothers,
people with weakened immune systems, the elderly, babies, and children, to avoid
dishes made with nuts and nut oils.

It is also prudent to check the labels of prepared ingredients for the possible inclusion
of nut derivatives.

The United States Department of Agriculture (USDA) advises that eggs should not
be consumed raw. This book contains some dishes made with raw or lightly cooked
eggs. It is prudent for more vulnerable people, such as pregnant and nursing mothers,
people with weakened immune systems, the elderly, babies, and young children, to
avoid uncooked or lightly cooked dishes made with eggs.

Contents

Introduction

30 20 10—Quick, Quicker, Quickest

This book offers a new and flexible approach to planning meals for busy cooks and lets you choose the recipe option that best fits the time you have available. Inside you will find 360 dishes that will inspire you and motivate you to get cooking every day of the year.

All the recipes take a maximum of 30 minutes to cook. Some take as little as 20 minutes and, amazingly, many take only 10 minutes. With a little preparation, you can easily try out one new recipe from this book each night and slowly you will build a wide and exciting portfolio of recipes to suit your needs.

How Does it Work?

Every recipe in the QuickCook series can be cooked one of three ways: a 30-minute version, a 20-minute version, or a superquick and easy 10-minute version. At the beginning of each chapter, you'll find recipes listed by time. Choose a dish based on how much time you have and turn to that page.

You'll find the main recipe in the middle of the page with a beautiful photograph and two time-variations below.

If you enjoy the dish, you can go back and cook the other time options. If you liked the 20-minute Bacon Carbonara (see pages 102–103), but only have 10 minutes to spare, then you'll find a way to cook it using quick ingredients or clever shortcuts.

If you love the ingredients and flavors of the 10-minute Herb Butter Squid (see pages 156–157), why not try something more substantial, such as the 20-minute Spiced Squid with Chickpeas, or be inspired to cook a more elaborate meal using similar ingredients, such as the 30-minute Crispy Squid. Alternatively, browse through all of the 360 delicious recipes, find something that catches your eye, and cook the version that fits your time frame.

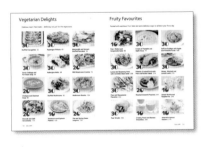

Or, for easy inspiration, turn to the gallery found on pages 12–19 to get an instant overview by themes, such as Vegetarian Delights or Fruity Favorites.

QuickCook Online

To make life even easier, you can use the special code on each recipe page to e-mail yourself a recipe card for printing, or e-mail a text-only shopping list to your phone. Go to www.hamlynquickcook.com and enter the recipe code at the bottom of each page.

 ITA-SOUP-MEJ

QuickCook Italian

There is much more to Italian food than you might first imagine. Pizza, pasta, and risotto are well known throughout Europe, and have been copied and reproduced (never at the same standard) for many years. But Italy has many different regions, each with its own special cuisine and eating habits.

The food in Italy has always been very important in society. The cuisine developed its diversity after the fall of the Roman Empire brought about a country of individually governed states that each had its own identity and, hence, its own traditions and cuisines. The true food of Italy is found in remote villages, where little has changed over the centuries. There, you will find country markets filled with produce that has been grown and picked by the person that is selling on the stall.

Geography also plays a large part in defining culinary styles, with around 1,500 miles of coastline where fish and seafood abound, plus the Apennine mountain range that forms the backbone of Italy. The length of the country allows for a huge variety of styles, with the north being more Germanic, cold-weather cooking using butter, and the south using more Mediterranean ingredients, with copious amounts of olive oil.

Other countries have also influenced Italian cuisine. The food of the northwest region of Italy bordering France closely resembles French cuisine (again using butter instead of olive oil), whereas the region bordering Austria in the northeast has Austrian influences and is known for its rich broths and smoked meats. Food in the south relies more heavily on seafood, with anchovies, sardines, and swordfish being widely used. Although the various regions serve different styles of food, there are some staple foods that are eaten across the country: pasta, risotto, and olive oil all feature extensively throughout Italy.

An Italian Meal

Italian cuisine starts with breakfast of a simple pastry and cup of coffee. Lunch is the main meal of the day and comprises several courses. Italian meals may last one or two hours, or even longer. Antipasti comes before a main meal and could consist of a platter of local meats, cheeses, stuffed bell peppers, and local breads. The first course is normally pasta, soup, or a rice dish, such as risotto. The second course is usually meat, poultry, or fish, and with this a side dish of potato, vegetables, or salad is served. Desserts or cheeses follow. Then the whole thing is rounded off by a good, strong Italian coffee.

Italians identify good food with fresh ingredients, and this also highlights the different regional dishes, because what grows well in Tuscany may not grow well in southern Italy. And although some ingredients are now available all year round, Italians prefer to create dishes using only seasonal ingredients. Regional recipes tend toward simplicity because they use only those ingredients that can be grown or sourced locally.

A Healthy Lifestyle

People who live in countries that border the Mediterranean Sea are known to have one of the healthiest diets in the world—locally grown fruit and vegetables, freshly caught fish and seafood, and everything drizzled with delicious olive oil (the Italian-Mediterranean diet is not low in fat, but olive oil is at least a healthy fat). Italians also take time to eat, enjoying family meals at a table—meal times are still very much a social occasion, all of which results in a healthier nation.

QuickCook Techniques and Tips

Creative cooking is not only for those who have plenty of time to spend in the kitchen. The recipes in this book can be cooked in relatively no time at all, using healthy, delicious ingredients and with a little help from a well-stocked pantry. The following pages feature a wide range of quick-to-prepare yet delicious Italian dishes, great for those of us who have a busy lifestyle. These recipes offer huge scope to be inventive in the quickest possible time. Using condiments, seasonings, herbs, and spices, can liven up your dining experience, giving you an opportunity to cook and eat a glorious palette of flavors, colors, and textures.

A well-equipped kitchen will help you to save time when preparing your meals. A couple of good saucepans of different sizes and a skillet are all essentials, and you will find plenty of uses for a good-quality mortar and pestle. A salad spinner speeds up salad washing, and accurate measuring equipment will help to make sure you have successful results. A food processor or blender is a must for preparing soups and sauces.

QuickCook Ingredients

Stock up on staples before you begin to travel through the varied and wonderful world of Italian cooking. With a good assortment of ingredients in your pantry, you can choose from a wider selection of speedy recipes to cook at a moment's notice.

pasta, polenta, rice, and beans

Pasta is eaten throughout Italy. It can be made with or without egg, using durum wheat and/or soft wheat flour and eaten fresh or dried. Italians have strong opinions regarding which pasta to use with which sauce, and different regions favor different combinations.

Polenta is a coarsely ground corn, similar to cornmeal, that is cooked in water to the consistency of mashed potatoes and served with meat or squid in a sauce. Once cold, soft polenta sets into a rigid block that can be topped with other ingredients and broiled. Instant polenta takes just five minutes to cook.

Risotto rice comes in three varieties—arborio, carnaroli, and vialone nano—all of which are grown in Italy's Po Valley. Stirring risotto as it cooks helps the grains release their starch and makes the final result deliciously creamy.

Cranberry beans, cannellini beans, chickpeas (garbanzo beans), and lentils are the basis of many Italian soups, stews, and salads. When cooking dried beans, first soak them overnight in cold water, then rinse before cooking them in fresh water. Canned beans, rinsed, can be used if time is short.

cheese and ham

Italy has many different types of cheese. Parmesan, perhaps the most celebrated of all, is a hard cheese made from cow milk in northern Italy used extensively in Italian cooking. Grana Padano is similar but more economical. Pecorino, made in central and southern Italy from sheep milk, is another popular choice. Fontina is a mild cheese from Piedmont, which melts smoothly, making it perfect for cooking. Of the blue cheeses, tasty Gorgonzola and milder, creamier dolcelatte are both used in creamy pasta sauces.

Softer cheeses also abound in Italy. Mozzarella can be made from cow or water buffalo milk; use the cow-milk type in cooking, but choose creamier buffalo mozzarella for eating fresh. Ricotta, which has many culinary uses, is a naturally low-fat soft cheese made from the whey left over from cheese making. Mascarpone—used in the classic dessert, tiramisu—is a thick, cream cheese with a rich, smooth texture and mild flavor.

Prosciutto is a dry-cured Italian ham, the most famous variety being Parma ham. It can be thinly sliced and served uncooked as an antipasti, but is equally versatile as a salad ingredient, or when used to wrap fillets of fish, meat, or chicken.

tomatoes
There is an abundance of tomatoes of every different kind available in Italy in summer and each variety has its own use. San Marzano plum tomatoes are prized for making sauces, and are the variety most commonly used in cans. The Italian "passata" is smooth, raw pureed tomatoes canned to be sold for cooking.

mushrooms
Porcini, chanterelles, and girolles are the most common wild mushrooms in Italy. During their short season in late summer and fall, they are eaten raw in salads, pan-fried with garlic and stirred into pasta, eaten on bruschette or polenta, used in risottos, or served with steak. Any other time of the year, Italians rely on dried mushrooms that need soaking in hot water before cooking.

anchovies, capers, and olives
These pantry favorites are invaluable for adding extra flavor to many Italian dishes. Anchovies are most commonly used in southern cooking, and can be bought fresh or preserved in salt or oil. Capers are small flower buds that are preserved in salt or brine (a salt solution). Olives are a staple of Italian cuisine, and are most often enjoyed as part of an antipasti, although they are also used to flavor everything from pizzas to pasta.

olive oil and vinegar
Olive oil comes in different grades: extra-virgin olive oil is made from the first cold pressing of olives and is rich in flavor, whereas regular, commercially processed olive oil is much milder. Because frying and sautéing can destroy the taste and fragrance of olive oil, use a cheaper, milder olive oil for cooking and reserve the more expensive type for uncooked dishes.

Red wine vinegar is commonly used in Italy for both dressing salads and cooking. Sweet and syrupy balsamic vinegar, made in Modena, is also popular, and just a few drops are enough to enliven a salad, sauce, or even a bowl of fresh strawberries.

Vegetarian Delights

Delicious meat-free treats—definitely not just for the vegetarians.

Stuffed Zucchini 32

Asparagus Frittata 40

Mozzarella and Spinach Stuffed Pancakes 52

Savoy Cabbage and Parmesan Soup 66

Eggplant Melts 68

Wild Mushroom Crostini 72

Chickpea and Chestnut Soup 86

Stuffed Mushrooms 92

Mushroom Risotto 104

Broccoli and Chili Orecchiette 114

Corn and Spinach Polenta 130

Pea and Scallion Linguine 150

Fruity Favorites

Packed with nutritious fruit, here are some delicious ways to achieve your five a day.

Pear, Walnut, and Gorgonzola Salad 60

Cream of Pumpkin and Apple Soup 74

Saffron Scallops with Apple and Pistachio Puree 180

Lemon and Rosemary Pork with Cannellini Bean Salad 206

Polenta-Crusted Pork with Pear and Arugula Salad 214

Honey, Mustard, and Lemon Lamb 216

Pear and Mascarpone Pancakes 242

Roasted Amaretti Peaches 244

Sweet Ricotta and Raspberries 246

Pear Strudel 256

Creamy Peach and Banana Smoothies 266

Amaretto Apricot Dessert 274

Summer Specials

Great ideas for alfresco dining, Italian style.

2 Sicilian Potato Salad 34

3 Wild Mushroom Tart 56

2 Grilled Swordfish with Salsa Verde 158

3 Mackerel with Beet and Potato Salad 162

1 Shrimp and Tomato Salad 184

2 Pan-Fried Red Snapper with Green Beans 186

3 Marinated Sardines 190

1 Tuna and Cannellini Bean Salad 192

1 Lamb-Stuffed Pita Pockets 208

1 Watermelon and Pineapple with Sambuca 258

2 Apple and Parmesan Tarts 264

3 Honeyed Fig Whips 270

Classics

Our selection of Italian classics, just like Mama used to make!

Peperonata 30

Potato Gnocchi 100

Bacon Carbonara 102

Fiorentina Pizza 106

Spaghetti Bolognese with Grilled Cherry Tomatoes 116

Spaghetti Puttanesca 136

Italian Fish and Seafood Stew 164

Beef Carpaccio 200

Creamy Veal Cutlets 224

Tiramisu 250

Zabaglioni 252

Biscotti 268

Entertaining

Make stressful dinner parties a thing of the past with these stunning, but easy dishes.

Antipasti with Breadsticks 24

Crab Linguine 110

Pea and Mint Risotto 118

Saffron Risotto 124

Rigatoni with Mussels and Zucchini 132

Herb Butter Squid 156

Monkfish Wrapped in Prosciutto with Lentils and Spinach 172

Creamy Mussels with Pancetta 182

Lamb and Olive Stew 198

Veal with Prosciutto and Sage 204

Mixed Peel Cassata 276

Chocolate Amaretti Puddings 278

Light and Healthy

Enjoy the fresh and light flavors of the Mediterranean.

Italian Vegetable Kebabs 54

Cranberry Bean and Roasted Red Pepper Bruschetta 62

Broiled Radicchio with Pancetta 76

Fava Bean and Mint Soup 84

Fusilli with Watercress, Raisins, and Pine Nuts 142

Stuffed Mussels 160

Shrimp and Cannellini Bean Salad 168

Tuna with Cannellini Beans and Roasted Red Pepper 174

Baked Trout with Olives 176

Sea Bass Fillets with Lentil Salad 178

Roman Chicken with Bell Peppers 218

Smoked Duck Breast Salad 234

Ways with Cheese

Where would Italian food be without cheese, in all its varied forms?

Parmesan Breadsticks 26

**Roasted Red Pepper and
Goat Cheese Salad** 38

**Spinach and Pecorino Balls
with Tomato Sauce** 42

Baked Ricotta 48

**Baked Fennel and
Gorgonzola** 70

Cheese-Stuffed Onions 78

Parmesan Crisps 82

**Fettucine with Dolcelatte
and Spinach** 122

**Cheese and Spinach
Calzones** 134

**Cheese Gnocchi with
Spinach and Walnuts** 146

Chicken Parmesan 202

**Ricotta Pancakes with
Oranges and Figs** 272

Ways with Tomatoes

A classic Italian ingredient, conjuring up the tastes of the sun.

Roasted Tomato Soup 46

Fava Beans with Anchovies and Tomatoes 50

Tomato, Basil, and Mozzarella Salad 58

Panzanella 80

Penne Arrabbiata 120

Tomato Risotto 128

Eggplant and Zucchini Ratatouille Pizzas 138

Margherita Pizza 148

Tuna in Tomato and Caper Sauce 166

Chili Cod in Tomato Sauce 170

Meatballs with Tomato Sauce and Spaghetti 222

Chicken BLT 226

QuickCook
Soups, Salads, and Light Bites

Recipes listed by cooking time

30

20

10

Antipasti with Breadsticks

Serves 4

1 cup marinated olives
4 chargrilled marinated artichokes
¼ cup chargrilled peppers
1 cup sun-dried tomatoes
1 (2 oz) can marinated anchovies
4 oz prosciutto
4 oz salami
8 oz mozzarella cheese
⅓ cup extra virgin olive oil
⅓ cup aged balsamic vinegar
grissini breadsticks, to serve

- Arrange the ingredients on a large platter or board. When ready to eat, pour the olive oil and balsamic vinegar into separate bowls for dipping.

- Serve the Antipasti with grissini breadsticks.

 Smoked Mackerel Bruschetta

Cut a large baguette into 8 slices. Brush each one with olive oil, and cook under a preheated hot broiler on both sides, until toasted and golden. Mix together 8 oz smoked mackerel with 6 chopped plum tomatoes, 2 tablespoons toasted pine nuts, the juice of 1 lemon, and 1 tablespoon chopped parsley. Stir ½ teaspoon creamed horseradish into ¾ cup cream cheese and spread the cheese onto each slice of bruschetta. Top with the mackerel mixture and serve.

Assorted Crostini

Cut a thin baguette into 12 slices. Brush each one with olive oil and cook under a hot broiler on both sides, until toasted and golden. Rub each slice with a garlic clove. Halve, core, and seed 1 red bell pepper and cook, cut side down, under a preheated hot broiler, until the skin turns black. Place in a bowl, cover with plastic wrap, and let stand until cool enough to handle, then peel away the blackened skin. Cut the peppers into strips and place on 4 of the crostinis. Top with ⅓ cup of crumbled goat cheese and ½ teaspoon chopped thyme leaves. Chop 1 tomato with ½ teaspoon capers and 4–5 basil leaves. Spoon this over another 4 of the crostini and drizzle with 1 tablespoon extra virgin olive oil. Top the remaining 4 crostini with 4 slices of prosciutto and 1 teaspoon capers.

30 Parmesan Breadsticks

Serves 4

1¾ cups white bread flour,
  plus extra for dusting
1¼ teapoons active dry yeast
½ teaspoon salt
½ tablespoon olive oil
about ⅔ cup warm water
½ cup finely grated Parmesan
  cheese

- Dust 2 baking sheets with flour. Place the flour, yeast, and salt in a bowl and mix together. Stir in the olive oil and 1–2 tablespoons of the measured water. Mix together with your hand, gradually adding more water, until you have a soft, but not sticky dough.

- Sprinkle over the grated Parmesan and knead the dough well until the cheese is completely incorporated.

- Turn the dough out onto a floured work surface and knead for 5–10 minutes, until the dough is smooth and elastic.

- Break into about 16 walnut-size pieces of dough and roll into long sticks. Place on the prepared baking sheets.

- Bake in a preheated oven, at 400°F, for 4–5 minutes, until golden and crisp. Let cool on a wire rack.

 Italian Flatbread
Place 2¼ cups all-purpose flour, 1 cup fine semolina, ½ teaspoon salt, and 1 tablespoon chopped rosemary in a bowl and mix together. Stir in 1–2 tablespoons of warm water. Mix together with your hand, gradually adding 1¼ cups warm water until you have a soft, but not sticky dough. Turn out onto a floured work surface and knead for 2–3 minutes. Divide into 8 pieces and roll out to 7–8 inch circles. Place the breads on 1 or 2 baking sheets dusted with flour. Bake in a preheated oven, at 425°F, for 2 minutes on each side.

 Garlic Bread
Soften 1½ sticks of butter and mix with 4–5 crushed garlic cloves and ¼ cup chopped parsley in a bowl. Halve a long baguette and then make ½ inch slits all the way along one of the halves, being careful not to cut all the way through the loaf (save the other half for another use). Spread each side of every slit in the loaf with the garlic butter mixture, pressing the loaf back together when finished. Wrap tightly in aluminum foil and bake in the oven at 400°F for 15–18 minutes, until golden and crisp.

3 Baked Mushrooms

Serves 4

8 large portabello mushrooms
3 tablespoons olive oil
8 thyme sprigs
2 tablespoons marsala wine
4 oz pancetta or chopped bacon
4 chestnuts, chopped
1 (6 oz) package spinach leaves
2 cups shredded mozzarella
  cheese
salt and pepper

- Place the mushrooms in an ovenproof dish, drizzle with 2 tablespoons of the olive oil, place a thyme sprig in each, and pour the marsala around the mushrooms. Bake in a preheated oven, at 400°F, for 15–18 minutes.

- Meanwhile, heat the remaining olive oil in a skillet and cook the pancetta for 4–5 minutes, until browned and just starting to crisp. Stir in the chopped chestnuts and spinach and stir until the spinach has wilted. Season well.

- Remove the mushrooms from the oven, spoon the filling into each one, and top with the shredded mozzarella. Return to the oven, or cook under a preheated hot broiler for 5–6 minutes, until the cheese is melted and golden.

---

1 Mushroom and Lentil Soup

Heat 2 tablespoons olive oil in a skillet and sauté 1 chopped onion and 2 sliced garlic cloves for 2–3 minutes. Add 2½ cups chopped cremini mushrooms and cook for 2–3 minutes. Stir in a drained 15½ oz can green lentils and 4 cups vegetable stock and bring to a boil. Simmer for 2–3 minutes and then stir in a small handful of chopped baby spinach leaves, 2 tablespoons chopped parsley, and 2 tablespoons grated Parmesan cheese. Serve with crusty bread.

2 Mushroom Penne

Put 1 lb sliced portobello mushrooms, 2 teaspoons whole-grain mustard, 4 crushed garlic cloves, a pinch of dried red pepper flakes, and 1¼ cups vegetable stock in a saucepan. Simmer for 10–12 minutes, until the stock has nearly all been absorbed. Meanwhile, cook 1 lb penne in a saucepan of boiling water according to the package directions, until "al dente." Drain the pasta and toss together with the mushrooms, grated rind of 1 lemon, 2 tablespoons chopped parsley, and 2 tablespoons grated Parmesan cheese. Serve with a crisp green salad.

ITA-SOUP-NOC

30 Peperonata

Serves 4

3 tablespoons olive oil

2 onions, sliced

2 garlic cloves, sliced

2 red bell peppers, cored, seeded, and cut into ½ inch slices

2 yellow bell peppers, cored, seeded, and cut into ½ inch slices

3 ripe tomatoes, diced

a small handful of basil leaves, shredded

- Heat the olive oil in a medium skillet and sauté the onion and garlic for 1–2 minutes.

- Add the bell peppers and cook over medium heat for another 10 minutes, then stir in the diced tomatoes.

- Continue to cook for 15 minutes, until the peppers have started to soften.

- Stir in the basil and serve.

Peperonata Salad
Toss together 2 red and 2 yellow cored, seededm and sliced bell peppers with 4 sliced tomatoes, a small handful of basil leaves, and 2 cups fresh baby spinach leaves. Sprinkle with 2 tablespoons olive oil and the juice of ½ lemon and toss again.

Quick Peperonata
Heat the olive oil in a medium skillet and add all the ingredients, except the basil leaves, as above. Cook for 15 minutes, stirring frequently. Serve sprinkled with chopped basil. This is a quicker, crunchier version of the above recipe.

3⦾ Stuffed Zucchini

Serves 4

4 zucchini
3 plum tomatoes, diced
2 cups shredded mozzarella
    cheese
2 tablespoons shredded basil
    leaves
¼ cup grated Parmesan cheese
salt and pepper

- Slice the zucchini in half horizontally and then scoop out the middle of each one, reserving the flesh.

- Place the zucchini halves in a roasting pan and bake in a preheated oven, at 400°F, for 10 minutes.

- Meanwhile, chop the reserved zucchini flesh and mix in a bowl with the diced tomatoes, shredded mozzarella, and basil. Season.

- Remove the zucchini halves from the oven and spoon the filling into each one.

- Sprinkle with the grated Parmesan and return to the oven to bake for 15 minutes, until golden.

 ### Zucchini and Lemon Salad

Grate 2 large zucchini into a salad bowl and toss together with 1 seeded and finely chopped red chile and 5–6 chopped basil leaves. Whisk together 2 tablespoons extra virgin olive oil, a squeeze of lemon juice, and ½ teaspoon honey in a small bowl. Pour the dressing over the zucchini and toss them together to coat with the dressing.

 ### Grilled Zucchini with Mozzarella

Use a vegetable peeler to thinly slice 4 zucchini lengthwise. Toss the zucchini in 2 tablespoons olive oil and then cook them on a preheated hot ridged grill pan for 2–3 minutes on both sides, until grill marks start to show. Served topped with 8 oz mozzarella cheese, torn, and 6–8 torn basil leaves. Drizzle with a little olive oil, a squeeze of lemon juice, and a grinding of pepper.

 # Sicilian Potato Salad

Serves 4

6–7 potatoes, peeled and chopped
1 teaspoon chopped oregano
2 garlic cloves, crushed
1 teaspoon red wine vinegar
3 tablespoons extra virgin olive oil
8 ripe plum tomatoes, diced
1 red onion, sliced
10–12 ripe black olives, pitted
4 hard-cooked eggs, sliced

- Cook the potatoes in a saucepan of boiling water for 12–15 minutes, until tender. Drain and cool slightly.

- Meanwhile, whisk together the oregano, garlic, red wine vinegar, and olive oil in a small bowl or jar and set aside until needed.

- Mix together the slightly cooled potatoes, the tomatoes, red onion, olives, and eggs in a large serving dish and drizzle with the dressing. Let stand for 2–3 minutes before serving.

 Sicilian Bean Salad

Make the Sicilian Potato Salad as above, replacing the potatoes with a 15 oz can of lima beans, rinsed and drained. Serve immediately.

 Sicilian Tuna and Potato Salad

Make the Sicilian Potato Salad as above. Toward the end of the potato cooking time, pan-fry 2 (5 oz) tuna steaks that have been seasoned with pepper for 4–5 minutes on each side, depending on how rare you like your tuna. Let rest for 2–3 minutes, then break up and gently toss into the potato salad.

Black Olive Tapenade on Toasted Ciabatta

Serves 4

3 tablespoons capers

4 anchovy fillets

1 garlic clove, crushed

juice of 1 lemon

2½ cups pitted ripe black olives

2 tablespoons chopped parsley

3–4 tablespoons olive oil

1 ciabatta loaf, sliced

salt and pepper

- Place the capers, anchovy fillets, garlic, and lemon juice in a food processor or blender and process for about 10 seconds, until you have a coarse puree.

- Add the olives, chopped parsley, and enough olive oil to make a paste. Process again, then season with salt and pepper.

- Toast the ciabatta slices on both sides. Spread each slice with tapenade and serve immediately.

2 Cod Loin with Black Olive Sauce

Put 2 cups coarsely chopped pitted black olives, ½ finely diced red chile, 2 tablespoons chopped basil leaves, 1 crushed garlic clove, the juice of 1 lemon, and 2–3 tablespoons olive oil in a bowl and mix to the consistency of a salsa. Heat 2 tablespoons olive oil in a skillet and cook 4 (5 oz) cod fillets for 3–4 minutes on each side, until cooked through. Spoon the olive sauce over the fish and serve with an arugula salad.

3 Asparagus and Tomatoes with Goat Cheese and Black Olives

Place 1 lb cherry tomatoes in a roasting pan, sprinkle with 2 tablespoons olive oil, and season. Add 4 halved garlic cloves and roast in a preheated oven, at 400°F, for 10 minutes. Spoon out some of the tomato juices, then add 12 oz asparagus spears. Return to the oven and cook for another 10 minutes. Meanwhile, cook 4 slices of goat cheese with rind under a preheated hot broiler for a few minutes, until slightly golden and soft. Serve the asparagus and tomatoes on 4 warm plates sprinkled with 1 cup pitted ripe black olives and topped with the broiled goat cheese.

ITA-SOUP-HYT

Roasted Red Pepper and Goat Cheese Salad

Serves 4

4 red bell peppers, halved, cored, and seeded

3 tablespoons extra virgin olive oil

juice of ½ lemon

1 teaspoon honey

1 teaspoon mustard

1 garlic clove, crushed

½ cup pine nuts

4 oz goat cheese

10–12 basil leaves

pepper

- Cook the red bell peppers, cut side down, under a preheated hot broiler for 8–10 minutes, until the skin turns black.

- Meanwhile, whisk together the olive oil, lemon juice, honey, mustard, and garlic in a small bowl or jar and season with pepper.

- Place the red bekk pepper in a large bowl, cover with plastic wrap, and let rest until cool enough to handle, then peel away the blackened skin.

- Toast the pine nuts, in a dry skillet, until they are golden.

- Cut the red bell peppers into strips and place on a platter. Crumble and scatter the goat cheese and the basil leaves over them and toss together gently.

- Drizzle with the dressing and serve sprinkled with the pine nuts.

 Red Pepper, Goat Cheese, and Arugula Salad Core, seed, and thinly slice 4 red bell peppers, then toss together with 2 cups arugula leaves, 8–10 shredded basil leaves, and 4 oz crumbled goat cheese in a salad bowl. Drizzle with 2 tablespoons extra virgin olive oil and 1 tablespoon balsamic vinegar and serve sprinkled with toasted pine nuts.

 Red Pepper and Goat Cheese Bruschetta Make the Red Pepper and Goat Cheese Salad as above. Cut a large baguette into slices. Drizzle with olive oil and cook under a preheated hot broiler on both sides, until toasted and golden. Rub each slice with a garlic clove. Divide the prepared salad mixture among the slices of bread and serve sprinkled with the toasted pine nuts.

ITA-SOUP-TYO

 Asparagus Frittata

Serves 4

12 oz asparagus
2 tablespoons olive oil
6 extra-large eggs
½ cup grated Parmesan cheese
1 tablespoon chopped oregano
salt and pepper

- Break the woody ends off the asparagus and discard. Toss the spears in 1 tablespoon of the olive oil.

- Heat a ridged grill pan or skillet until hot and cook the asparagus for 4–5 minutes, until starting to look a little charred. Cut the asparagus spears into thirds.

- Beat the eggs in a large bowl with the grated Parmesan, oregano, and some salt and pepper. Add the asparagus.

- Heat the remaining oil in a flameproof, nonstick skillet. Pour the mixture into the skillet and cook for 8–10 minutes over low heat, tipping the skillet from time to time to let the runny egg reach the edges to cook.

- Cook for another 4–5 minutes under a preheated hot broiler, until the top is golden.

- Turn out onto a chopping board, cut into wedges, and serve immediately.

 Grilled Asparagus
Toss 1 lb trimmed asparagus in 2 tablespoons olive oil. Heat a ridged grill pan until hot and cook the asparagus for 4–5 minutes, turning once. Serve drizzled with olive oil and sprinkled with Parmesan cheese shavings.

Asparagus Omelets
Steam 12 oz trimmed asparagus for 2–3 minutes, until tender. Meanwhile, whisk together 8 eggs and some salt and pepper in a large bowl with a tiny splash of water. Heat a small skillet (or omelet pan if you have one) and melt 1 tablespoon of butter. Pour in one-quarter of the egg mixture. Cook for 1 minute, tipping the skillet from time to time to let the runny egg reach the edges to cook, then let cook until the omelet is just set. Sprinkle one-quarter of the asparagus over half of the omelet and fold the other side over the asparagus. Slide onto a warm plate. Repeat with the remaining egg and asparagus to make 4 omelets.

30 Spinach and Pecorino Balls with Tomato Sauce

Serves 4

8 oz baby spinach leaves
1 egg, beaten
1 garlic clove, crushed
½ cup grated Pecorino cheese
1½ cups fresh bread crumbs
1 tablespoon olive oil
2 shallots, diced
1 (14½ oz) can diced tomatoes
¼ cup red wine
2 tablespoons shredded basil
  leaves
vegetable oil, for frying
salt and pepper
¼ cup grated Parmesan cheese,
  to serve

- Steam the spinach for 1–2 minutes, until wilted. Squeeze out any excess moisture and coarsely chop.

- Mix the spinach with the egg, garlic, Pecorino, bread crumbs, and some salt and pepper in a bowl.

- Roll the mixture into walnut-size balls and chill for 15 minutes.

- Meanwhile, make the tomato sauce. Heat the olive oil in a saucepan and sauté the shallots for 2–3 minutes. Pour in the diced tomatoes and red wine and add the basil. Simmer for 8–10 minutes.

- Heat vegetable oil in a deep skillet until it is 350–375°F, or until a cube of bread browns in 30 seconds when dropped into the oil.

- Working in batches, cook the spinach balls for 3–4 minutes, until they are golden. Remover with a slotted spoon and drain on paper towels.

- Serve with the tomato sauce and a good sprinkling of grated Parmesan.

 Spinach and Pecorino Salad

Whisk together 3 tablespoons extra virgin olive oil, 1 tablespoon balsamic vinegar, 1 teaspoon Dijon mustard, and ½ teaspoon honey. Toss together 6 oz baby spinach leaves, 3 tablespoons toasted pine nuts, 2 tablespoons golden raisins, and 1 cored, seeded, and thinly sliced red bell pepper. Toss in the dressing along with ¼ cup Pecorino shavings.

 Spinach and Pecorino Pasta

Cook 1 lb spiral pasta shapes in a saucepan of boiling water according to the package directions, until "al dente." Meanwhile, heat 1 tablespoon olive oil in a skillet and sauté 2 diced shallots for 3–4 minutes. Stir in ½ cup ricotta cheese, 12 quartered cherry tomatoes, and 3½ cups baby spinach leaves and mix well. Drain the pasta and stir into the sauce. Serve sprinkled with 3 tablespoons grated Pecorino cheese.

 # Layered Potatoes and Mushrooms

Serves 4

butter, for greasing
4 russet potatoes,
  peeled and thinly sliced
10 oz cremini or porcini
  mushrooms, thinly sliced
1 large onion, thinly sliced
½ cup olive oil
3 tablespoons chopped parsley
1 cup fresh bread crumbs
½ cup grated Parmesan cheese
salt and pepper

- Grease an ovenproof dish or roasting pan. Blanch the potatoes in a saucepan of boiling water for 2–3 minutes and then drain.

- Layer the potatoes, mushrooms, and onion in the greased ovenproof dish, drizzling each layer with olive oil and sprinkling with chopped parsley.

- Season well and sprinkle over the bread crumbs and Parmesan. Bake in a preheated oven, at 400°F, for 22 minutes, until the potato is completely cooked and the topping is golden.

10 Garlicky Mushrooms with Mashed Potatoes

Heat 3 tablespoons olive oil and 2 tablespoons butter in a skillet and sauté 3 crushed garlic cloves for 1–2 minutes. Add 10 oz sliced cremini mushrooms and cook for 4–5 minutes. Meanwhile, heat a 24 oz container of store-bought prepared mashed potatoes according to the package directions. Stir 1 tablespoon chopped parsley into the mushrooms and serve spooned over the potatoes. Serve drizzled with 1 tablespoon olive oil.

Bean, Potato, and Mushroom Salad

Cook 8 oz new potatoes in a saucepan of boiling water for about 12–15 minutes, until tender. Add 2 cups green beans for the last 3 minutes of cooking. Drain and refresh under cold running water, put in a serving bowl, and toss in 3 tablespoons olive oil. Add 1 sliced red onion, 1 tablespoon capers, and 8 halved cherry tomatoes. Heat 2 tablespoons olive oil in a skillet and cook 4 oz diced pancetta and 1 cup diced cremini mushrooms, until the pancetta is crisp. Sprinkle over the salad to serve.

# Roasted Tomato Soup

Serves 4

2 lb ripe tomatoes, halved
4 garlic cloves, unpeeled
2 tablespoons olive oil
1 onion, chopped
1 carrot, chopped
1 celery stick, sliced
1 red bell pepper, cored, seeded,
  and chopped
3 cups hot vegetable stock
salt and pepper
¼ cup grated Parmesan cheese,
  to serve

- Place the tomato halves and garlic cloves in a roasting pan. Sprinkle with 1 tablespoon of the olive oil and some pepper and roast in a preheated oven, at 400°F, for 20 minutes.

- After 10 minutes, heat the remaining olive oil in a saucepan and sauté the onion, carrot, celery, and red bell pepper over low heat for 10 minutes.

- When the tomatoes are cooked, remove the garlic cloves in their skins and squeeze the garlic flesh into the pan with the sautéed vegetables.

- Pour in the roasted tomatoes and all the juices along with the stock. Using a handheld blender, or in a food processor or blender, blend the soup until smooth. Season to taste.

- Reheat, if necessary, then serve sprinkled with the grated Parmesan.

Quick Tomato Toasts

Toast 4 slices of bread on both sides, then rub each slice with a garlic clove and sprinkle with shredded basil leaves. Slice 4 tomatoes and place the tomato slices on top of the basil. Sprinkle with 1 cup shredded mozzarella cheese and cook under a preheated hot broiler until the cheese is bubbling and golden.

Quick Tomato Soup

Heat 2 tablespoons olive oil in a saucepan and sauté 1 chopped onion, 1 chopped carrot, 1 celery stick, and 6 chopped tomatoes for 5 minutes. Pour in a 14½ oz can diced tomatoes and 3¾ cups hot vegetable stock. Simmer for 10 minutes, remove from the heat, and add a small handful of basil leaves. Using a handheld blender, or in a food processor or blender, blend the soup until smooth. Season to taste and serve with an extra drizzle of olive oil.

30 Baked Ricotta

Serves 4

2 cups ricotta cheese
grated rind of 1 lemon
4 eggs, beaten
½ cup grated Parmesan cheese
1 teaspoon finely chopped thyme
  leaves
1½ lb baby spinach leaves
4 ripe tomatoes, diced
pepper
2 teaspoons extra virgin olive oil,
  to serve

- Beat together the ricotta, lemon rind, eggs, Parmesan, and thyme in a bowl and season with pepper. Spoon into 4 ramekin dishes.

- Bake in a preheated oven, at 375°F, for 20–22 minutes, until risen and lightly golden.

- Meanwhile, steam the spinach for 1–2 minutes, until wilted, then divide among 4 plates.

- Let the baked ricotta cool for 1–2 minutes. Run a knife around the outside and then turn each one out onto a bed of steamed spinach.

- Sprinkle with the diced tomatoes and serve drizzled with the olive oil.

---

1 **Quick Ricotta Dip**
Stir 2 tablespoons store-bought prepared pesto and 2 tablespoons toasted pine nuts into 1 cup of ricotta cheese in a bowl. Core and seed 2 red and 2 yellow bell peppers, slice them into thin strips, and serve with the dip.

2 **Ricotta-Stuffed Pasta Shells**
Cook 1 lb conchiglioni in a saucepan of boiling water according to the package directions, until "al dente." Meanwhile, chop 3 seeded tomatoes and mix with 2 cups ricotta cheese and 2 tablespoons shredded basil. Place a spoonful of the ricotta mixture into each pasta shell and lay them in a greased ovenproof dish. Drizzle with 2 tablespoons olive oil and sprinkle with 2 tablespoons grated Parmesan cheese. Place under a preheated hot broiler for 2–3 minutes. Serve with a salad.

Fava Beans with Anchovies and Tomatoes

Serves 4

8½ cups fresh or frozen
fava beans (2½ lb)
3 tablespoons olive oil
1 lb cherry tomatoes, halved
6 scallions, sliced
2 garlic cloves, finely sliced
6 anchovy fillets, chopped
1 tablespoon shredded basil
leaves
1 tablespoon chopped parsley
2 cups arugula leaves
2 tablespoons Parmesan cheese
shavings, to serve

· Blanch the fava beans in a saucepan of boiling water for
1 minute and then refresh under cold water. Drain and peel
off the outer skins.

· Heat the olive oil in a skillet and cook the tomatoes over
medium heat for 4–5 minutes.

· Add the scallions and garlic and cook for another 1–2 minutes,
then add the fava beans.

· Stir in the anchovies and herbs and cook for 1–2 minutes.

· Spoon into a large serving bowl, toss with the arugula
leaves, and serve topped with Parmesan shavings.

Mashed Lima Beans and Anchovy

Heat 2 (15 oz) cans lima beans,
rinsed and drained, in a saucepan
of boiling water for 2–3 minutes
and then drain. Process together
½ chopped red chile and
4 anchovy fillets in a food
processor or blender. Pour
in the warm lima beans and
process until coarsely chopped.
Stir in a small handful of chopped
parsley, the juice of ½ lemon,
and 2–3 tablespoons olive oil to
make chunky mashed lima beans.
Great served with broiled lamb.

Roasted Peppers with Tomatoes

and Anchovies Place 4 halved,
cored, and seeded bell peppers,
cut sides up, in a roasting pan.
Halve 8 tomatoes and divide
among the bell peppers. Top
each one with 1–2 anchovy
fillets, a few slices of garlic, and
a few rosemary sprigs. Drizzle
with 2–3 tablespoons olive oil,
season with pepper, and bake
in a preheated oven, at 400°F,
for 22–25 minutes.

ITA-SOUP-PAB

30 Mozzarella and Spinach Stuffed Pancakes

Serves 4

1 cup all-purpose flour
a pinch of salt
2 eggs
1 cup milk mixed with ¼ cup water
4 tablespoons butter, melted
1 (6 oz) package baby spinach leaves
4 tomatoes, sliced
12 oz mozzarella cheese, sliced
2 tablespoons grated Parmesan cheese

- To make the batter, sift the flour and salt into a large bowl. Make a well in the center and break the eggs into it. Beat the eggs into the flour and then gradually add a small amount of the milk and water, still beating.

- Beat half the melted butter into the pancake batter and use the remainder to grease a skillet. Rub the skillet with paper towels to remove any excess.

- Pour about 2 tablespoons of the batter into the skillet and swirl around to completely coat the bottom. After about 1 minute check that the pancake is cooked underneath, then flip it over to cook the other side for just a few seconds.

- Sprinkle half the pancake with some spinach leaves, sliced tomatoes, and sliced mozzarella. Fold the other half of the pancake over the filled side and press lightly. Transfer the filled pancake to an ovenproof dish and keep warm.

- Repeat with the remaining ingredients. Sprinkle the pancakes with the grated Parmesan and briefly cook under a preheated hot broiler until golden. Serve immediately.

 Mozzarella and Spinach Salad

Layer 3½ cups spinach leaves with 12 oz sliced mozzarella cheese, 2 thinly sliced beefsteak tomatoes, and 10–12 basil leaves on a large platter. Sprinkle with 2 teaspoons chopped oregano and 2 tablespoons toasted pine nuts and drizzle with 3 tablespoons extra virgin olive oil and 1 tablespoon balsamic vinegar.

 Mozzarella and Spinach Pizza

Place 2 large prepared pizza crusts on 2 baking sheets and spread with 2 cups tomato puree. Heat 2 tablespoons olive oil in a large skillet and sauté 2 sliced garlic cloves and 1 sliced red onion for 2–3 minutes, then stir in 1 lb baby spinach leaves. Continue to stir until the spinach has completely wilted. Spread the wilted spinach over the pizza crusts, then sprinkle with 2 cups shredded mozzarella cheese, 1 tablespoon chopped basil leaves, and some pepper. Bake in a preheated oven, at 400°F, for 12–15 minutes, until the cheese is melted and golden.

 Italian Vegetable Kebabs

Serves 4

2 red bell peppers, cored, seeded, and chopped

1 yellow bell pepper, cored, seeded, and chopped

2 zucchini, cut into thick slices

1 large red onion, cut into wedges

2 tablespoons olive oil

2 tablespoons lemon juice

2 tablespoons torn basil leaves

salt and pepper

- Place the chopped vegetables in a large bowl and toss in the olive oil, lemon juice, basil, and salt and pepper.

- Thread the vegetables onto metal skewers and broil or barbecue over medium heat for 10–12 minutes, turning occasionally, until cooked. Serve immediately.

Grilled Vegetables Thickly slice 3 zucchini lengthwise, and core, seed, and thickly sliced 2 red and 2 yellow bell peppers. Heat a ridged grill pan until hot and cook the vegetables for about 4–5 minutes, until charred and starting to soften. Place on a platter and sprinkle with 3 tablespoons Parmesan cheese shavings and 2 tablespoons shredded basil leaves. Drizzle with Italian salad dressing to serve.

Italian Vegetable Kebabs with Herb Pasta Cook 10 oz tagliatelle according to the package directions, until "al dente." When cooked, drain the pasta and toss with 2 tablespoons torn basil leaves and 2 tablespoons olive oil. Meanwhile, heat 1 tablespoon olive oil in a skillet and cook 1 diced red chile and 1 diced garlic clove for 1 minute, then add 1½ cups small white button mushrooms, 1 red bell pepper, cored, seeded, and cut into chunks, and 1 sliced zucchini. Cook for 2–3 minutes. Thread the vegetables onto soaked wooden skewers with 4 oz Muenster cheese cubes and 3 thickly sliced scallions. Cook under a preheated hot broiler for 2–3 minutes to heat through. Serve the kebabs on a bed of the herbed pasta.

30 Wild Mushroom Tart

Serves 4

1 sheed rolled dough pie crust

⅓ oz dried porcini

2 tablespoons olive oil

1 red onion, sliced

12 oz mushrooms (include a variety of wild and cremini)

2 eggs, beaten

½ cup mascarpone cheese

1 teaspoon thyme leaves

2 teaspoons whole-grain mustard

½ cup grated Parmesan cheese

pepper

- Use the pie crust to line a 9 inch tart pan. Chill for 5 minutes.

- Soak the porcini in a bowl with enough boiling water to just cover them.

- Heat the olive oil in a skillet and cook the onion and mushrooms for 5 minutes, stirring frequently.

- Beat together the eggs, mascarpone, and thyme leaves in a bowl and season with pepper.

- Drain and chop the porcini and add to the egg, along with the mushrooms from the skillet. Mix well.

- Spread the mustard over the bottom of the pie crust. Pour in the mushroom mixture and level with the back of a spoon.

- Sprinkle with the grated Parmesan and bake in a preheated oven, at 400°F, for 20 minutes, until golden. Slice into generous pieces and serve hot or cold.

1 Mushroom and Taleggio

Bruschetta Heat 2 tablespoons olive oil in a skillet and sauté 4 oz wild mushrooms with 1 crushed garlic clove for 4–5 minutes. Stir in 1 tablespoon chopped parsley. Toast 8 slices of large baguette on both sides. Top each slice of bread with the mushroom mixture and then a slice of taleggio cheese. Cook under a preheated hot broiler for 1–2 minutes, until the cheese is bubbling. Serve warm.

2 Wild Mushroom Ragout with

Polenta Heat 2 tablespoons olive oil in a skillet and cook 12 oz mixed wild mushrooms with 2 crushed garlic cloves for 2–3 minutes. Stir in 1 tablespoon chopped tarragon, 1 tablespoon chopped thyme leaves, and a drizzle of truffle oil (optional). Bring 3½ cups water to a boil and add 1¼ cups instant polenta. Cook, stirring continuously, for 1 minute, then stir in 2 tablespoons butter and some salt and pepper. Spread the polenta in the bottom of an ovenproof dish and pour over the mushroom mixture. Dab with 8 oz chopped taleggio cheese and cook under a preheated hot broiler, until the cheese is melted and golden.

Tomato, Basil, and Mozzarella Salad

Serves 4

3 tablespoons extra virgin
 olive oil
juice of ½ lemon
1 teaspoon honey
1 teaspoon mustard
1 garlic clove, crushed
7 ripe tomatoes
1 lb mozzarella cheese, sliced
10–12 basil leaves, shredded
pepper

- Whisk together the olive oil, lemon juice, honey, mustard, garlic, and some pepper in a bowl.

- Place the tomatoes in a large bowl and pour over boiling water. Let stand for 30 seconds, then drain and refresh under cold water. Peel off the skins and slice the tomatoes.

- Layer the tomatoes with slices of mozzarella and torn basil leaves on plates or a large serving bowl.

- Drizzle with the dressing and let stand for 5 minutes before serving.

 Speedy Tomato and Mozzarella Salad Thinly slice 14 ripe plum tomatoes (1¾ lb) and layer on a platter with 1 lb sliced mozzarella cheese and 10–12 basil leaves. Drizzle with olive oil and balsamic vinegar and serve.

 Tomato and Mozzarella Tart Roll out 1 sheet chilled store-bought, ready-to-bake puff pastry on a lightly floured work surface to 10 inches square. Place on a baking sheet and score a square about 1 inch in from the edge. Bake in a preheated oven, at 400°F, for 10 minutes, until golden. Slice 6 ripe tomatoes and 8 oz mozzarella cheese and place these, slightly overlapping, in the center square, letting the edge remain risen. Top with about 10–12 basil leaves and sprinkle with 2 tablespoons pine nuts. Bake for another 10–12 minutes, until the cheese is melted and the pastry is golden. Serve with 2 cups arugula leaves in 2 tablespoons olive oil and 1 tablespoon balsamic vinegar.

1⃝ Pear, Walnut and Gorgonzola Salad

Serves 4

3 tablespoons extra virgin olive oil

1 teaspoon Dijon mustard

1 tablespoon white wine vinegar

1 teaspoon superfine or granulated sugar

⅓ cup walnut pieces

1 radicchio, leaves separated

2 cups arugula leaves

1 romaine heart, leaves separated and torn

2 pears, cored and sliced

1½ cups crumbled Gorgonzola or other blue cheese

- Whisk together the olive oil, mustard, vinegar, and sugar in a small bowl.

- Toast the walnut pieces in a dry skillet, until golden, to help bring out their flavor.

- Toss together the radicchio, arugula, and romaine heart leaves in a bowl. Divide the leaves among 4 plates and sprinkle with the slices of pear, crumbled Gorgonzola, and the walnuts.

- Pour the dressing over the salad and serve.

 Gorgonzola with Warm Marsala Pears Place 4 (3½ oz) slices of Gorgonzola cheese in a serving dish. Core and cut 2 pears into eighths. Heat 1 tablespoon olive oil in a skillet and cook the pears for 3–4 minutes on each side. Whisk together 2 tablespoons honey and 2 tablespoons marsala wine, then pour into the skillet, letting it simmer and thicken for a few minutes. Using a slotted spoon, remove the pears and place them on top of the Gorgonzola. Sauté ½ cup walnut halves in the remaining syrup in the skillet. Pour the syrup and walnuts over the pears and Gorgonzola to serve.

 Pear, Walnut, and Gorgonzola Pizza Heat 1 tablespoon olive oil in a skillet and sauté 1 large sliced red onion for about 4–5 minutes, until softened. Add 2 cored and sliced pears. Stir in 2 tablespoons balsamic vinegar and some pepper and cook until the onions start to caramelize. Spread 4 prepared pizza crusts with 2 tablespoons tomato puree, then divide the pear mixture between the crusts. Top each one with 2 cups crumbled Gorgonzola cheese and ½ cup walnuts. Bake in a preheated oven, at 400°F, for 10–12 minutes.

Cranberry Bean and Roasted Red Pepper Bruschetta

Serves 4

1 large baguette, cut into 8 slices
3 tablespoons olive oil
1 garlic clove
1 (15½ oz) can cranberry beans, rinsed and drained
3 scallions, sliced
½ cup finely sliced, drained roasted red peppers from a jar
6 basil leaves, thinly shredded
salt and pepper

- Place the baguette slices on a baking sheet and drizzle with 2 tablespoons of the olive oil. Cook under a preheated hot broiler for 2–3 minutes on each side, until toasted and golden.

- Rub each slice of toast with the garlic clove.

- Place the drained cranberry beans and scallions in a bowl and lightly crush together with a fork.

- Stir in the red pepper, basil, remaining olive oil, and some salt and pepper.

- Spoon the bean mixture onto the toasted baguette slices and serve immediately.

Quick Bean Salad In a large serving bowl, mix together a 15½ oz can cranberry beans, rinsed and drained, 3 sliced scallions, ½ cup chopped, drained roasted red peppers from a jar, 3 diced tomatoes, 4–5 shredded basil leaves, 2 tablespoons olive oil, and 1 tablespoon balsamic vinegar.

Bean and Roasted Red Pepper Salad Halve, core, and seed 4 red bell peppers and cook, cut side down, under a preheated hot broiler, until the skin turns black. Place in a large bowl, cover with plastic wrap, and let stand until they are cool enough to handle. Meanwhile, whisk together 3 tablespoons extra virgin olive oil, the juice of ½ lemon, 1 teaspoon Dijon mustard, and ½ teaspoon sugar. Toss together 1 torn romaine lettuce, 1 small red onion, peeled and thinly sliced, 8 halved cherry tomatoes, 2 tablespoons coarsely chopped parsley, and a 15½ oz can cranberry beans, rinsed and drained. When the peppers are cool enough to handle, peel away the blackened skin and cut into strips. Toss these with the other salad ingredients. Cook 4 slices of goat cheese with rind under a hot broiler for 3–4 minutes, until slightly golden and soft. Divide the salad among 4 plates or shallow bowls and top each one with a slice of broiled goat cheese. Drizzle with the dressing and serve sprinkled with 1 tablespoon chopped oregano leaves.

20 Arancini

Serves 4

5 cups cold spinach risotto, either leftover or store-bought prepared (1½ lb)

4 oz mozzarella cheese, cut into cubes

2 eggs, beaten

3 cup fresh bread crumbs

3–4 cups peanut oil

arugula leaves, to serve

- Using wet hands, take a small handful of cold risotto and roll into a ball. Press a cube of mozzarella into the middle of the ball and seal by squeezing the rice around it. Repeat with the remaining risotto and mozzarella to make about 12 balls.

- Place the beaten egg in one shallow bowl and the bread crumbs in another. Dip each ball into first the egg and then the bread crumbs to coat completely.

- Pour the peanut oil into a deep-fat fryer or large saucepan, and heat until it is 350–375°F, or until a cube of bread browns in 30 seconds when dropped into the oil. Working in batches, cook the arancini for 3–4 minutes, until golden. Remove with a slotted spoon and drain on paper towels.

- Serve hot with arugula leaves.

10 Rice Salad

Gently toss together 3 cups store-bought precooked long grain rice, 1 (8 oz) can asparagus tips, 1 cored, seeded, and chopped red bell pepper, 2 tablespoons chopped sun-dried tomatoes, the grated rind and juice of 1 lemon, 2 tablespoons extra virgin olive oil, 8 oz halved mini mozzarellas, and a large handful of shredded basil leaves. Season well and serve.

30 Rice with Chicken

Heat 2 tablespoons olive oil in a saucepan and brown 2 boneless, skinless chicken breasts, sliced into strips, for 3–4 minutes. Add 2 thickly sliced red onions, 3 sliced garlic cloves, and 3 cored, seeded, and thickly sliced red bell peppers and cook for another 4–5 minutes. Stir in 1 cup long-grain rice, a 14½ oz can diced tomatoes, and 2 cups chicken stock. Bring to a boil and then transfer to and ovenproof dish. Bake in a preheated oven, at 400°F, for 15–18 minutes, until the stock is absorbed and the rice and chicken are cooked. Serve sprinkled with 2 tablespoons grated Parmesan cheese.

Savoy Cabbage and Parmesan Soup

Serves 4

¼ cup olive oil
1 onion, chopped
2 garlic cloves, crushed
½ teaspoon fennel seeds
1 savoy cabbage
1 potato, diced
4 cups vegetable stock
¾ cup grated Parmesan cheese,
   plus extra 1 tablespoon to serve
salt and pepper
crusty bread, to serve

- Heat 2 tablespoons of the olive oil in a saucepan and sauté the onion, garlic, and fennel seeds for 3–4 minutes.

- Shred 4 leaves of the cabbage and reserve. Finely shred the remaining cabbage, add to the pan with the diced potato, and cook for 3–4 minutes, then pour in the stock.

- Simmer for 10 minutes, until the potato is tender. Stir in the grated Parmesan.

- Using a handheld blender, or in a food processor or blender, blend the soup until smooth. Season to taste.

- Heat the remaining olive oil and stir-fry the reserved cabbage. Top each bowl of soup with the fried cabbage.

- Serve sprinkled with extra grated Parmesan, and slices of crusty bread on the side.

 Coleslaw with Italian Dressing

Whisk together 3 tablespoons extra virgin olive oil, 1 tablespoon white wine vinegar, 1 tablespoon chopped parsley, ½ tablespoon lemon juice, 1 crushed garlic clove, ½ teaspoon dried basil, and a pinch of dried oregano. In a large bowl, shred ½ green cabbage, 2 carrots, and ½ onion and mix with the dressing to serve.

 Rice with Savoy Cabbage

Heat 3 tablespoons olive oil in a skillet and sauté 1 chopped onion for 2–3 minutes. Stir in 5 cups finely shredded savoy cabbage and cook, stirring, until wilted. Stir in 1⅓ cups risotto rice and 4 cups beef stock. Bring to a boil and simmer for 15–16 minutes, until the rice is "al dente". Stir in 2 tablespoons butter and ½ cup grated Parmesan, season, and serve.

ITA-SOUP-QAO

30 Eggplant Melts

Serves 4

2 eggplants, halved lengthwise
¼ cup olive oil
4 tomatoes, sliced
8 oz mozzarella cheese, sliced
a small handful of basil leaves
2 tablespoons toasted pine nuts
pepper
crisp green salad, to serve

- Place the eggplant halves on a baking sheet, drizzle with the olive oil, and bake in a preheated oven, at 400°F, for 20 minutes, until softened.

- Remove the eggplant from the oven, arrange the slices of tomato and mozzarella on top, and bake for another 5 minutes, until the cheese has melted.

- Sprinkle with basil leaves and pine nuts, season with pepper, and serve with a crisp green salad.

1 Eggplant Dip and Caramelized Onion

Bruschetta Heat 1 tablespoon olive oil in a skillet and cook 1 sliced onion over low heat for 6 minutes, stirring occasionally, until the onion starts to caramelize. Sprinkle in ½ teaspoon sugar and 1 teaspoon balsamic vinegar and cook for another minute. Toast 8 slices of ciabatta on both sides, then spread with prepared eggplant dip. Spoon the caramelized onions over the toasts to serve.

2 Eggplant and Goat Cheese Pasta

Cook 12 oz pasta shapes of your choice in a saucepan of boiling water according to the package directions, until "al dente." Meanwhile, heat 1 tablespoon olive oil in a skillet and sauté 1 chopped onion and 2 sliced garlic cloves for 3–4 minutes. Add 1 chopped eggplant and cook for another 4–5 minutes. Pour in a 14½ oz can diced tomatoes and simmer for 3–4 minutes. Drain the pasta and stir into the sauce with ⅔ cup crumbled goat cheese and a small handful of torn basil leaves and mix well.

 # Baked Fennel and Gorgonzola

Serves 4

4 fennel bulbs
3 tablespoons olive oil
8 oz Gorgonzola or other
  blue cheese
pepper

- Trim the fennel bulbs and slice vertically.

- Heat the oil in a skillet and sauté the fennel for 2–3 minutes, then transfer to an ovenproof dish.

- Break the Gorgonzola into chunks and sprinkle them over the fennel.

- Bake in a preheated oven, at 400°F, for 25 minutes, until the fennel is tender and has turned slightly golden at the edges.

 Quick Fennel Coleslaw

Mix together 2 fennel bulbs, 2 large carrots, 1 small onion, all finely sliced, with ½ tablespoon chopped parsley, 1 tablespoon mayonnaise, and the juice of ½ lemon.

 Gorgonzola Croutons with Fennel and Orange Salad

Peel and segment 2 oranges over a bowl to catch the juice. Whisk the orange juice with 3 tablespoons extra virgin olive oil, 2 teaspoons honey, and 1 teaspoon whole-grain mustard. Toast 3 tablespoons pumpkin seeds in a dry skillet until golden. Toss together the orange segments, 2 finely sliced fennel bulbs, 1½ cups watercress, and the dressing. For the croutons, cut a baguette into 8 slices. Toast each slice on one side under a preheated hot broiler, then turn over and top with 6 oz Gorgonzola cheese. Cook until the cheese is bubbling and golden. Divide the salad among 4 plates and top each one with 2 Gorgonzola croutons. Sprinkle with the toasted pumpkin seeds before serving.

ITA-SOUP-JIJ

Wild Mushroom Crostini

Serves 4

2 thin baguettes

¼ cup olive oil

2 garlic cloves, 1 whole, 1 crushed

1 shallot, diced

4 oz mixed wild mushrooms, chopped

1 tablespoon chopped parsley

pepper

- Cut the baguettes into slices diagonally, about 1 inch thick. Place the slices on a baking sheet and brush with 2 tablespoons of the olive oil.

- Bake in a preheated oven, at 400°F, for 4–5 minutes, until golden brown. Rub each slice with the whole garlic clove and keep the slices warm.

- Heat the remaining oil in a skillet and sauté the shallot and crushed garlic for 3–4 minutes, then add the mushrooms and cook them until they have released all of their juices. Stir in the chopped parsley and season with pepper.

- Spoon the mushroom mixture onto the crostini and serve.

Wild Mushroom Omelet

Heat 1 tablespoon olive oil and 2 tablespoons butter in an omelet pan and sauté ½ small sliced onion for 1–2 minutes. Stir in 4 oz wild mushrooms and cook for 2–3 minutes. Pour in 6 beaten eggs with ½ tablespoon chopped tarragon, tipping the pan from time to time to let the runny egg reach the edges to cook. When almost cooked, carefully fold over one side of the omelet and slide onto a warm plate. Divide into 2 to serve. Repeat with the same ingredients to make another omelet to be divided into 2. Serve with a green salad.

Asparagus and Wild Mushroom

Pasta Cook 12 oz pasta in a saucepan of boiling water according to the package directions, until "al dente." Meanwhile, heat 1 tablespoon olive oil in a skillet and sauté 1 lb trimmed and halved asparagus for 3–4 minutes. Pour in ¼ cup vegetable stock, ½ teaspoon dried red pepper flakes, and 8 oz wild mushrooms (if wild not available, normal portobello mushrooms can be used). Cook for 4–5 minutes. Drain the pasta and gently toss in the asparagus mixture. Serve sprinkled with 2 tablespoons grated Parmesan cheese.

ITA-SOUP-QAW

3⦿ Cream of Pumpkin and Apple Soup

Serves 4

2 tablespoons olive oil

1 onion, chopped

4 cups cubed pumpkin flesh

1 Granny Smith apple, peeled, cored, and chopped

2 tomatoes, skinned and chopped

3¾ cups vegetable stock

½ cup heavy cream

1 tablespoon finely chopped parsley

salt and pepper

- Place the tomatoes in a large bowl and pour over boiling water. Let stand for 30 seconds, then drain and refresh under cold water. Peel off the skins and dice the tomatoes.

- Heat the olive oil in a large saucepan and sauté the onion for 3–4 minutes.

- Add the pumpkin and stir to coat with the onions. Stir in the apple and the diced tomatoes.

- Pour in the stock, bring to a boil, and then simmer, covered, for 20 minutes, until the pumpkin is tender.

- Let the soup cool a little before pouring in the cream. Using a handheld blender, or in a food processor or blender, blend the soup until smooth.

- Gently reheat if necessary, season, and serve immediately, sprinkling in the chopped parsley.

1⦿ Pumpkin Hummus

Blend together

1 cup canned pumpkin puree, 3 tablespoons tahini, 1–2 crushed garlic cloves, a 15 oz can chickpeas (garbanzo beans), rinsed and drained, 1 tablespoon lemon juice, and ½ teaspoon ground cumin in a food processor or blender. Gradually add olive oil until you have the consistency you like. Add salt and pepper to taste and serve with vegetable crudités.

2⦿ Pumpkin and Chickpea Salad

Toss 8 cups diced pumpkin flesh with 1 crushed garlic clove, ½ teaspoon ground cumin, and 2 tablespoons olive oil and roast in a preheated oven, at 400°F, for 15 minutes. Mix the roasted pumpkin with a 15 oz can chickpeas (garbanzo beans), rinsed and drained, 1 small diced red onion, 1 cup crumbled feta cheese, ¼ cup sun-dried tomatoes, and 2 cups arugula leaves. Serve dressed with Italian salad dressing.

 Broiled Radicchio with Pancetta

Serves 4

2 tablespoons olive oil
½ tablespoon balsamic vinegar
3 garlic cloves, crushed
1 tablespoon chopped rosemary
2 radicchio heads, cut into
    quarters through the core end
8 pancetta slices
pepper
Pecorino cheese shavings,
    to serve

- Whisk together the olive oil, vinegar, garlic, and rosemary in a large nonmetallic bowl and season with pepper. Add the radicchio and toss to coat. Let stand for 10 minutes.

- Wrap each quarter of radicchio with a slice of pancetta.

- Cook the radicchio under a preheated hot broiler or on a hot barbecue grill for 5–6 minutes, until the edges are crisp and slightly charred, turning occasionally.

- Serve on a platter drizzled with the remaining marinade and sprinkled with Pecorino shavings.

Radicchio Slaw

Cook 2 oz diced pancetta under a preheated hot broiler until crisp. Meanwhile, mix together 1 thinly sliced radicchio head, 2 carrots, and 1 fennel bulb, both cut into matchsticks, 2 tablespoons mayonnaise, the juice of ½ lemon, and some salt and pepper. Sprinkle with the crisp pancetta to serve.

Radicchio Risotto

Heat 2 tablespoons olive oil in a saucepan and sauté 2 finely chopped onions with 2 oz diced pancetta for 3–5 minutes. Add 1 shredded radicchio head and cook for 2–3 minutes. Stir in 1½ cups risotto rice until the edges of the grains look translucent. Pour in 1 cup white wine and cook for 1–2 minutes, until it is all absorbed. Add a ladle from 3¼ cups hot chicken stock and stir continuously, until it has all been absorbed. Repeat with the remaining hot stock, adding a ladle at a time, until the rice is "al dente." Remove from the heat and stir in 2 tablespoons butter and ¼ cup grated Parmesan cheese. Serve sprinkled with an extra 2–3 tablespoons grated Parmesan.

ITA-SOUP-FIS

 # Cheese-Stuffed Onions

Serves 4

4 large onions, peeled
5 cups spinach leaves
½ cup ricotta cheese
1 egg yolk
1 teaspoon chopped thyme leaves
1 oz Fontina cheese
½ cup grated Parmesan cheese
2 tablespoons butter

To serve

2 cups arugula leaves
3 tablespoons balsamic syrup

- Blanch the onions in boiling water for 5 minutes. Drain and let cool for 5 minutes.

- Meanwhile, heat 1 tablespoon olive oil in a large saucepan, cook the spinach until wilted, and then coarsely chop. Place in a bowl with the ricotta, egg yolk, thyme, Fontina, and ¼ cup of the grated Parmesan.

- Slice off the top of each onion and remove the middle sections with a fork.

- Spoon the cheese mixture into the onions and place them in a roasting pan. Sprinkle with the remaining grated Parmesan, dab with butter, and roast in a preheated oven, at 400°F, for 15 minutes, until the cheese is bubbling and golden.

- Serve on a bed of arugula leaves, drizzled with balsamic syrup.

1 Cheese and Onion Bruschetta

Heat 1 tablespoon olive oil in a skillet and sauté 1 large sliced onion for 2–3 minutes, until soft. Stir in ½ teaspoon sugar and 1 teaspoon balsamic vinegar and cook for another 1–2 minutes. Toast 8 slices of ciabatta on both sides. Top each one with the caramelized onions and ½ cup crumbled Gorgonzola cheese. Cook under a preheated hot broiler until the cheese is golden and bubbling.

2 Onion Soup

Heat 2 tablespoons olive oil in a saucepan and cook 4 crushed garlic cloves, 4 sliced red onions, 2 sliced white onions, 4 sliced shallots, and 3–4 sage leaves, covered, for 10–12 minutes, stirring occasionally. Sprinkle in 1 teaspoon sugar and 1 teaspoon balsamic vinegar and season well. Pour in 8 cups hot vegetable or chicken stock and simmer for 4–5 minutes. Serve with slices of cheese on toast.

30 Panzanella

Serves 4

2 ripe tomatoes

1 ciabatta roll

16 olives, pitted

3 teaspoons capers

½ red onion, finely sliced

16 red and yellow cherry
    tomatoes, halved

6–8 basil leaves

1 tablespoon red wine vinegar

2 tablespoons olive oil

- Place the tomatoes in a strainer over a bowl. Using the back of a spoon, squash them well to release all the juice into the bowl.

- Roughly break up the roll and add it to the tomato juice. Let stand for 15 minutes, then transfer to a serving dish.

- Sprinkle the remaining ingredients over the bread, drizzling with the red wine vinegar and olive oil before serving.

---

1 Tomato Ciabatta Toasts

Toast 8 slices of ciabatta on both sides, then rub each slice with a garlic clove. Top the ciabatta slices with 2 cups diced tomatoes and 2 teaspoons capers. Sprinkle with chopped basil leaves and drizzle with olive oil.

2 Tomato Salad with Ciabatta Croutons

Cut 1 ciabatta loaf into cubes. Heat 2 tablespoons olive oil in a skillet and sauté the cubes of bread until they are golden. Drain on paper towels. Toss the fried bread together with 3 coarsely chopped ripe tomatoes, 16 pitted ripe black olives, ½ sliced red onion, 16 red and yellow cherry tomatoes, 6–8 torn basil leaves, and 2 cups baby spinach leaves. Drizzle with 2 tablespoons olive oil and 1 tablespoon red wine vinegar to serve.

10 Parmesan Crisps

Serves 4

2 cups grated Parmesan cheese

- Line 2 or 3 baking sheets with parchment paper. Place a 2 inch pastry cutter on the baking sheet and sprinkle 1 heaping teaspoon of the grated Parmesan inside the cutter to make a circular disk.

- Carefully remove the cutter and repeat with the remaining cheese, leaving ¼ inch between each disk.

- Bake in a preheated oven, at 325°F, for 8 minutes, until golden brown.

- Using a spatula, transfer the crisps to a wire rack to cool.

- Store in an airtight container until required.

 2 Parmesan Biscuits

Put 1¾ cups all-purpose flour, 2¾ teaspoons baking powder, 4 tablespoons butter, and ¼ cup grated Parmesan cheese in a food processor and process until it resembles fine bread crumbs. Add ⅔ cup milk and process until the dough comes together. Turn out onto a lightly floured work surface and gently roll or press out to a thickness of ¾ inch. Cut out 8 biscuits using a 2½ inch pastry cutter. Place them on a baking sheet, sprinkle with 2 tablespoons grated Parmesan, and bake in a preheated oven, at 425°F, for 12–15 minutes, until golden.

 3 Parmesan and Thyme Shortbread

Cream 6 tablespoons butter in a mixing bowl and then add ¾ cup all-purpose flour, 1 cup grated Parmesan cheese, 2 teaspoons olive oil, and 1½ teaspoons chopped thyme leaves. Using your hands, bring the mixture together into a dough. Roll the dough out on a lightly floured work surface to a thickness of ¼ inch and cut out 18–20 circles using a 1¾–2 inch pastry cutter. Place the circles on a baking sheet and chill for 15 minutes. Bake in a preheated oven, at 350°F, for 7–8 minutes, until lightly golden.

 # Fava Bean and Mint Soup

Serves 4

4 cups frozen fava beans, defrosted

2 tablespoons olive oil

2 shallots, peeled and diced

1 large carrot, peeled and diced

1 celery stick, diced

3¾ cups vegetable stock

½ tablespoon chopped mint leaves

salt and pepper

¼ cup heavy cream, to serve

- Blanch the fava beans in boiling water for 3–4 minutes, then drain and refresh under cold water. Peel off the tough outer skins.

- Meanwhile, heat the olive oil in a saucepan and sauté the shallots, carrot, and celery for 5–6 minutes. Stir in the skinned fava beans.

- Pour in the stock, bring to a boil, and then simmer for 8–10 minutes.

- Stir in the mint and then, using a handheld blender, or in a food processor or blender, blend the soup until smooth.

- Season to taste and serve with a swirl of cream.

Fava Bean Dip

Blanch 3 cups fava beans in boiling water for 3–4 minutes, then drain and refresh under cold water. Peel off the outer skins then place in a food processor or blender with 1 chopped red onion and a handful of mint leaves. Blend together. Stir in 1½ cups crème fraîche or sour cream, the juice of ½ lemon, and some salt and pepper. Serve with toasted ciabatta slices.

Fava Bean, Pea, and Mint Salad

Blanch 2 cups fava beans and 1¹/₃ cups peas in a saucepan of boiling water for 3–4 minutes, then drain and refresh under cold water. Peel off the tough outer skins from the fava beans. Heat 2 tablespoons extra virgin olive oil in a skillet and sauté 2 handfuls of cubed bread, 2 crushed garlic cloves, and 2 teaspoons chopped basil leaves until the croutons are golden. Drain on paper towels. Heat a ridged grill pan until hot and cook 8 oz sliced Muenster cheese until it has marks on both sides. Whisk together 3 tablespoons extra virgin olive oil, 1 tablespoon balsamic vinegar, 1 teaspoon whole-grain mustard, and ½ teaspooon honey in a bowl. Toss the fava beans and peas with 2 tablespoons shredded mint leaves, 2 cups arugula leaves, and the croutons. Top with the grilled Muenster cheese and drizzle with the dressing to serve.

Chickpea and Chestnut Soup

Serves 4

1 tablespoon olive oil

2 celery sticks, chopped

2 garlic cloves, chopped

1 red chile, seeded and chopped

1 teaspoon chopped rosemary

1 (14½ oz) can diced tomatoes

12 oz of vacuum-packed chestnuts

1 (15 oz) can chickpeas (garbanzo beans), rinsed and drained

1¾ cups vegetable stock

salt and pepper

To serve

2 tablespoons olive oil

2 tablespoons grated Parmesan cheese

- Heat the olive oil in a saucepan and sauté the celery, garlic, chile, and rosemary for 2–3 minutes.

- Stir in the tomatoes, chestnuts, and chickpeas with the stock and simmer for 8–10 minutes.

- Remove one-third of the soup and blend, using a handheld blender, or in a food processor or blender, to produce a thick consistency. Return to the pan, season, and serve with a swirl of olive oil and sprinkled with grated Parmesan.

Chickpea, Chestnut, and Feta Salad

Drain and rinse a 15 oz can chickpeas (garbanzo beans), and toss with ½ diced red chile, 2 shredded Boston lettuce, 6 quartered cherry tomatoes, 4 chopped vacuum-packed chestnuts, 1 cored, seeded, and diced red bell pepper, and 1⅓ cups crumbled feta cheese. Toss with 2–3 tablespoons Italian salad dressing and serve with crusty bread.

Pork Loin Chops with Chestnut

Sauce Heat 2 tablespoons olive oil in a skillet and cook 4 oz diced pancetta for 4–5 minutes, then add ¼ cup red wine and 7 oz of chopped vacuum-packed chestnuts. Pour in ⅔ cup chicken stock and cook for 10–12 minutes, until the chestnuts are soft and breaking down. Blend the sauce in a food processor or blender and season to taste. Meanwhile, cook 1 chopped potato and 1 small chopped sweet potato in a saucepan of boiling water until tender. Add a 15 oz can chickpeas (garbanzo beans), drained and rinsed, for the last 2 minutes of cooking to heat through. Drain and coarsely crush with a fork. Cook 4 (5 oz) pork chops under a preheated hot broiler for 3–4 minutes on each side and serve on top of the crushed potatoes with the chestnut sauce spooned over them and sprinkled with torn sage leaves.

30 Eggplant Parmigiana

Serves 4

3 tablespoons olive oil

2 eggplants, sliced

1 onion, diced

2 garlic cloves, crushed

1 (14½ oz) can diced tomatoes

1 teaspoon chopped oregano

2 cups shredded mozzarella cheese

2 beefsteak tomatoes, thinly sliced

⅓ cup grated Parmesan cheese

- Heat 2 tablespoon of the olive oil in a skillet and cook the eggplant slices in batches, until golden.

- Heat the remaining oil in the skillet and sauté the onion and garlic for 3–4 minutes. Stir in the tomatoes and oregano.

- Layer the eggplant slices in an ovenproof dish with the mozzarella and beefsteak tomatoes.

- Pour the tomato sauce over the layers and sprinkle with the grated Parmesan. Bake in a preheated oven, at 400°F, for 15–18 minutes. Serve warm.

 Zucchini and Tomato Gratin

Heat 2 tablespoons olive oil in a pan and sauté 3 sliced zucchini until golden. Layer with 4 sliced tomatoes, 6–8 coarsely torn basil leaves, and 2 cups shredded mozzarella in an ovenproof dish. Sprinkle with 2 tablespoons bread crumbs and ¼ cup grated Parmesan. Bake in a preheated oven, at 425°F, for 5 minutes.

 Ricotta-Stuffed Eggplant Rolls

Heat a ridged grill pan. When hot, grill slices of eggplant that have been cut lengthwise from 2 eggplants, for 2–3 minutes on each side, until golden. Mix together ½ cup ricotta cheese, 1½ cups shredded mozzarella cheese, 2 teaspoons chopped basil leaves, and 2 sliced scallions. Place 1 teaspoon of the ricotta mixture onto the end of each slice of eggplant, then roll up each slice and place seam side down in an ovenproof dish. Pour 1 cup prepared tomato sauce over the rolls and bake in a preheated oven, at 375°F, for 12–15 minutes, until the cheese starts to melt. Serve with a arugula salad.

Zucchini Fritters with Poached Eggs

Serves 4

4 zucchini, shredded
¼ cup all-purpose flour
½ teaspoon baking powder
½ cup grated Parmesan cheese
2 tablespoons olive oil
4 eggs
pepper

- Place the shredded zucchini, flour, baking powder, and grated Parmesan in a bowl and mix together well.

- Squeeze into walnut-size balls and then gently flatten.

- Heat the oil in a deep skillet and, working in batches if necessary, cook the fritters for 2–3 minutes on each side, until golden.

- Meanwhile, bring a large saucepan of water to a gentle simmer and stir with a large spoon to create a swirl. Carefully break 2 eggs into the water and cook for 3 minutes. Remove with a slotted spoon and keep warm. Repeat with the remaining eggs.

- Serve the fritters topped with the poached eggs and sprinkled with pepper.

 Grilled Zucchini with Mint and Lemon

Use a vegetable peeler to slice 4 zucchini very thinly, brush each slice with olive oil, and sprinkle with 2 crushed garlic cloves. Heat a ridged grill pan until very hot and cook the slices for 2–3 minutes on each side, until charred (this can also be done on a hot barbecue grill). Place on a serving platter and sprinkle the grated rind and juice of 1 lemon and 1 finely chopped green chile over them. Toss gently. To serve, drizzle with 1 tablespoon olive oil and sprinkle with 2 tablespoons chopped mint leaves and ¼ cup Parmesan shavings.

 Zucchini and Parmesan Soup

Heat 3 tablespoons olive oil in a saucepan and sauté 6 zucchini (2 lb), chopped, with 2 chopped garlic cloves and a small handful of chopped basil leaves. Pour in 3¼ cups vegetable stock and bring to a boil. Simmer for 8–10 minutes and then remove from the heat. Stir in ¼ cup light cream. Using a handheld blender, or in a food processor or blender, blend the soup until smooth. Stir in ½ cup grated Parmesan cheese, season with pepper, and reheat. Serve with crusty bread.

30 Stuffed Mushrooms

Serves 4

2 tablespoons olive oil

2 shallots, finely diced

1 garlic clove, crushed

1 (6 oz) package fresh spinach leaves

1 cup store-bought prepared long-grain rice

¼ cup chopped Gorgonzola or other blue cheese

4 large portabello mushrooms, stems trimmed

2 tablespoons grated Parmesan cheese

crisp green salad, to serve

- Heat 1 tablespoon of the olive oil in a skillet and sauté the shallot and garlic for 2–3 minutes.

- Stir in the spinach and cook until it has wilted. Remove from the heat and stir in the rice and Gorgonzola and mix well.

- Place the mushrooms in a roasting pan and divide the spinach mixture among them. Sprinkle with the grated Parmesan.

- Drizzle with the remaining olive oil and bake in a preheated oven, at 400°F, for 18–20 minutes, until cooked.

- Serve with a crisp green salad.

---

10 Creamy Mushroom Toasts

Toast 8 slices of ciabatta on both sides, then rub each slice with a garlic clove. Heat 2 tablespoons olive oil in a skillet and sauté 3 sliced scallions and 10 oz cremini mushrooms for 3–4 minutes, until softened and just starting to brown. Stir in 1 tablespoon chopped parsley and 1 tablespoon crème fraîche, then spoon the mixture over the ciabatta slices and serve.

20 Fennel and Tomato Stuffed

Mushrooms Heat 2 skillets, each with 1 tablespoon olive oil. In one skillet, place 4 portabello mushrooms that have had the stems removed. Cook over a low heat for 12–15 minutes. Meanwhile, cook the chopped mushroom stems, 1 diced fennel bulb, 3 diced tomatoes, and 3 sliced garlic cloves in the other skillet for 5–6 minutes. Stir in 2 tablespoons bread crumbs, ¾ cup crumbled Gorgonzola or other blue cheese, and a small handful of shredded basil leaves. Spoon the mixture into the mushrooms and place on a baking sheet. Sprinkle with 2 tablespoons grated Parmesan cheese and cook under a preheated hot broiler until golden.

QuickCook

Pizza, Pasta, and More

Recipes listed by cooking time

Quick Artichoke and Salami Pizzas

Serves 4

4 flour tortillas
1½ cups tomato puree
8 oz salami, sliced
1 (14 oz) can artichoke hearts, drained and sliced
6 sliced scallions, sliced
1 teaspoon dried oregano
2 cups shredded mozzarella

- Place the tortillas on 2 baking sheets and warm in a preheated oven, at 425°F, for 2 minutes.

- Remove from the oven and spread each tortilla with tomato puree and then top each one with some salami, sliced artichoke hearts, scallions, oregano, and mozzarella.

- Bake the pizzas for another 3–5 minutes, until the tortilla edges are lightly browned and the mozzarella has melted.

---

2 **Orecchiette with Artichoke and Salami** Cook 16 oz orecchiette in a saucepan of boiling water according to the package directions, until "al dente." Meanwhile, heat 1 tablespoon olive oil in a saucepan and add 4 oz sliced salami, cut into strips, for 1–2 minutes. Stir in a 14½ oz can diced tomatoes, ½ cup vegetable stock, and a 14 oz can artichoke hearts, drained and halved. Simmer for 5–6 minutes. Drain the pasta and add it to the salami sauce. Serve sprinkled with grated Parmesan cheese.

3 **Artichoke and Red Pepper Pizza** Place 7⅓ cups white bread flour, 1½ tablespoons active dry yeast, and a pinch of salt in a large bowl and mix together. Stir in 2 tablespoons olive oil and about 2½ cups warm water and mix together, using your hands, until you have a soft but not sticky dough. Turn out the dough onto a floured work surface and knead for 5–8 minutes. Divide into 4 pieces and roll out to 12 inch circles, then place on baking sheets. Spread each one with ⅓ cup tomato puree, then divide a 14 oz can artichoke hearts and ¾ cup roasted red peppers from a jar, both drained and sliced, among the pizzas. Sprinkle with 2 cups shredded mozzarella cheese and cook in a preheated oven, at 425°F, for 6–7 minutes.

ITA-PIZZ-POX

30 Potato Gnocchi

Serves 4

7 russet potatoes (1¾ lb), peeled
and diced
1 egg yolk, beaten
1¼ cups all-purpose flour
⅓ cup finely shredded basil leaves
½ cup grated Parmesan cheese
¼ cup extra virgin olive oil
salt and pepper

- Cook the potatoes in a saucepan of boiling water for 12–15 minutes, until soft. Drain and mash, or use a potato ricer to get a really smooth texture. Place another saucepan of water on the heat to boil.

- Transfer the mashed potato to a bowl and mix in the egg yolk, flour, and basil. Mix well to combine.

- Take a teaspoon of the mixture into your hand and roll into a walnut-size ball. Press with the prongs of a fork to make a gnocchi shape. Repeat with the remaining mixture.

- Drop the gnocchi into the saucepan of boiling water to cook—this should take only 1–2 minutes, and the gnocchi will float when cooked.

- Toss the hot gnocchi in the grated Parmesan and olive oil and serve immediately.

1 Potato Gnocchi in a Quick Tomato Sauce

Heat 1 tablespoon olive oil in a skillet and sauté 2 diced shallots and 2 crushed garlic cloves for 1–2 minutes. Add a 14½ oz can diced tomatoes, a pinch of dried red pepper flakes, 2 teaspoons thyme leaves, and 2 tablespoons white wine. Simmer for 5–6 minutes. Meanwhile, cook 1¾ lb store-bought prepared gnocchi for 2 minutes in a saucepan of boiling water. Drain and toss the cooked gnocchi in the tomato sauce and serve sprinkled with Parmesan cheese shavings.

2 Potatoes with Pancetta and Capers

Cook 8 chopped russet potatoes (2 lb) in a saucepan of boiling water until tender. Meanwhile, heat 2 tablespoons olive oil and 2 tablespoons butter in a skillet and sauté 1 chopped onion and 4 oz diced pancetta for 5–6 minutes. Stir in 1 tablespoon chopped rosemary and 2 tablespoons capers. Drain the potatoes, add to the caper mixture, and lightly crush in the pan. Bring a large saucepan of water to a gentle simmer and stir with a large spoon to create a swirl. Carefully break 2 eggs into the water and cook for 3 minutes. Remove with a slotted spoon and keep warm. Repeat with another 2 eggs. Stir 1 tablespoon chopped basil into the potatoes and divide among 4 warm bowls. Top each one with a poached egg and sprinkle with 2 tablespoons grated Parmesan cheese.

Bacon Carbonara

Serves 4

16 oz spaghetti
2 tablespoons butter
3 garlic cloves, finely diced
2 shallots, finely diced
8 bacon slices, chopped
4 eggs
1 cup light cream
½ cup grated Parmesan cheese

- Cook the spaghetti in a saucepan of boiling water according to the package directions, until "al dente."
- Meanwhile, heat the butter in a large skillet and sauté the garlic, shallots, and bacon for 5–7 minutes, until golden.
- Beat together the eggs, cream, and half the grated Parmesan.
- Using tongs, transfer the cooked spaghetti to the skillet— don't worry if some of the cooking liquid comes with it.
- Pour in the egg mixture and toss the spaghetti until well coated, adding more cooking liquid, if necessary.
- Serve sprinkled with the remaining Parmesan.

---

10 Quick Bacon and Egg Spaghetti

Cook 16 oz thin spaghetti in a saucepan of boiling water according to the package directions, until "al dente." Meanwhile, heat 1 tablespoon olive oil in a skillet and cook 8 chopped bacon slices until crisp. Beat together 4 eggs, 1 cup light cream, and ½ cup grated Parmesan cheese in a bowl. Drain the pasta, then return to the pan and add the egg mixture and bacon. Toss together until the spaghetti is well coated. Season with salt and pepper and serve sprinkled with extra grated Parmesan.

30 Bacon and Pine Nut Pasta with Poached Eggs

Bring a large saucepan of water to a gentle simmer and stir with a large spoon to create a swirl. Carefully break 2 eggs into the water and cook for 3 minutes. Remove with a slotted spoon and repeat with another 2 eggs. Keep them warm. Cook 16 oz tagliatelle in a saucepan of boiling water according to the package directions, until "al dente." Meanwhile, heat 1 tablespoon olive oil in a skillet and sauté 6 oz bacon slices, cut into strips, for 2 minutes. Add 1⅓ cups frozen peas, 2 tablespoons vegetable stock, ¼ cup crème fraîche or sour cream, and 4 sliced scallions. Stir well and bring to a gentle simmer. Continue to cook for 3–4 minutes. Drain the pasta, transfer to the skillet, and gently toss in the creamy bacon sauce. Divide the pasta among 4 shallow bowls and top each one with a poached egg. Serve sprinkled with 2 tablespoons grated Parmesan and pepper.

30 Mushroom Risotto

Serves 4

1/3 oz dried porcini
1 cup boiling water
1 tablespoon olive oil
2 shallots, diced
2 cups risotto rice
2/3 cup white wine
2½ cups hot stock
6 oz cremini mushrooms
1 teaspoon chopped thyme leaves
salt and pepper
2 tablespoons grated Parmesan
   cheese, to serve

- Place the dried porcini in a bowl and cover with the measured water. Let stand for 15 minutes.

- Meanwhile, heat the olive oil in a saucepan and sauté the shallots for 2–3 minutes, unitl softened but not browned.

- Stir in the rice and continue to stir, until the edges of the grains look translucent.

- Pour in the wine, and cook for 1–2 minutes over high heat and stir until it is absorbed.

- Add a ladle of the hot stock, reduce the heat to medium, and stir continuously until it has been absorbed. Repeat with the remaining hot stock, a ladle at a time.

- Drain the porcini, reserving the liquid. Coarsely chop the porcini and add to the rice with the fresh mushrooms and a ladle of the porcini liquid.

- Continue to stir and add liquid, until the rice is "al dente."

- Stir in the thyme and season to taste. Serve sprinkled with grated Parmesan.

 Quick Mushroom Rice

Heat 2 tablespoons olive oil in a skillet and saute 12 oz cremini mushrooms and 4 sliced scallions for 5–6 minutes. Stir in a 3 cups cooked rice and 1 tablespoon chopped parsley. Season and serve sprinkled with 2 tablespoons grated Parmesan.

 Rice and Mushroom Soup

Heat 2 tablespoons olive oil in a saucepan and sauté 2 chopped leeks and 2 sliced garlic cloves for 4–5 minutes, until softened. Add 10 oz chopped cremini mushrooms, ¼ cup long-grain rice, and 2 teaspoons thyme leaves and cook for another 2–3 minutes. Pour in 5 cups hot vegetable stock and simmer for 5 minutes. Using a handheld blender, or in a food processor or blender, blend the soup until smooth. Season to taste and serve with crusty bread.

Fiorentina Pizzas

Serves 4

2 large store-bought pizza crusts

2 cups tomato puree

2 tablespoons olive oil

2 garlic cloves, sliced

1 red onion, sliced

1 lb fresh spinach leaves

4 eggs

2 tablespoons pine nuts

2 cups shredded mozzarella
  cheese

pepper

- Place the pizza crusts on 2 baking sheets and spread each one with tomato puree.

- Heat the olive oil in a large skillet and sauté the garlic and onion for 2–3 minutes, then add the spinach and stir until it has completely wilted.

- Spread the wilted spinach over the pizza crusts and make 2 small hollows in each pizza topping. Break the eggs into the hollows.

- Sprinkle each pizza with pine nuts, mozzarella, and pepper.

- Bake in a preheated oven, at 400°F, for 12–15 minutes, until the eggs are cooked. Cut into slices and serve immediately.

---

10 **Healthy Pita Pizzas**

Lightly poach 4 eggs. Toast 4 whole wheat pita breads under a preheated hot broiler for 1–2 minutes on each side, then spread with 1 tablespoon ketchup. Heat 1 tablespoon olive oil in a skillet, add 12 oz fresh spinach leaves, and sauté until wilted. Spread the spinach over the pita breads. Top each one with a poached egg, then sprinkle with 1 tablespoon each of pine nuts and shredded mozzarella. Cook under the hot broiler for 3–4 minutes, until the cheese melts.

30 **Homemade Fiorentina Pizzas**

Mix together 7⅓ cups white bread flour, 1½ tablespoons active dry yeast, and a pinch of salt. Stir in 2 tablespoons olive oil and 1–2 tablespoons warm water. Mix together with your hand, gradually adding about 2½ cups warm water, until you have a soft but not sticky dough. Turn out the dough onto a lightly floured work surface and knead for 5–8 minutes, until the dough is smooth and elastic. Divide into 4 pieces and roll into 12 inch circles, then place on 2 baking sheets. Heat 2 tablespoons olive oil in a skillet, add 1 lb fresh spinach leaves, and sauté until wilted. Spread 2 cups tomato puree over the pizza crusts, followed by the spinach. Crack an egg into the center of each pizza, sprinkle wiht 2 cups shredded grated mozzarella cheese and cook in a preheated oven, at 425°F, for 6–7 minutes, until the eggs are cooked.

Pappardelle with Creamy Asparagus and Herbs

Serves 4

1 lb asparagus, trimmed and cut into 1 inch lengths

16 oz pappardelle

1 tablespoon olive oil

1 onion, diced

2 garlic cloves, crushed

1¼ cups light cream

¼ teaspoon grated nutmeg

2 tablespoons each of chopped basil, parsley and chives

2 tablespoons grated Parmesan cheese, to serve

- Blanch the asparagus in a saucepan of boiling water for 3–4 minutes. Drain and keep warm.

- Cook the pappardelle in a saucepan of boiling water according to the package directions, until "al dente."

- Meanwhile, heat the olive oil in a skillet and sauté the onion and garlic for 4–5 minutes.

- Stir in the cream and simmer for 6–8 minutes, until the cream has reduced and thickened a little. Stir in the grated nutmeg.

- Drain the pasta and add to the cream sauce with the asparagus and herbs. Toss together gently.

- Serve sprinkled with grated Parmesan.

 Asparagus Pasta Salad

Cook 8 oz fresh penne in a saucepan of boiling water according to the package directions, until "al dente," then drain and refresh under cold water. Meanwhile, steam 12 oz halved asparagus tips until tender, then drain and refresh under cold water. Place the pasta and asparagus in a salad bowl and toss together with 6 chopped cherry tomatoes, ¾ cup roasted red peppers from a jar, drained and sliced, 1 cup chopped mozzarella cheese, 1 tablespoon chopped basil leaves, and some Italian salad dressing.

 Asparagus Pesto Pasta

Cook 16 oz tagliatelle in a saucepan of boiling water according to the package directions, until "al dente." Meanwhile, cook 1 lb trimmed asparagus in a saucepan of boiling water for 2–3 minutes, then drain. Place the asparagus, 4 cups spinach leaves, ¼ cup grated Parmesan cheese, 2 crushed garlic cloves, and 2 tablespoons toasted pine nuts in a food processor and process for 30 seconds, then pour in 3–4 tablespoons extra virgin olive oil with the motor still running until a thick paste forms. Add the juice of ½ lemon and a little water to loosen and season to taste. Drain the pasta, return to the pan, and add the asparagus pesto. Toss together. Serve sprinkled with extra toasted pine nuts.

20 Crab Linguine

Serves 4

16 oz linguine
½ cup olive oil
2 garlic cloves, crushed
1 red chile, seeded and
　finely diced
grated rind and juice of 1 lemon
8 oz white crab meat
2 tablespoons chopped parsley

- Cook the linguine in a large saucepan of boiling water according to the package directions, until "al dente."

- Meanwhile, in another large saucepan, heat the olive oil and cook the garlic, chile, and lemon rind over low heat for 3–4 minutes.

- Drain the pasta and add it to the olive oil pan along with the lemon juice, crab meat, and the chopped parsley. Toss together gently to warm the crab through and then serve.

10 Crab Pasta Salad

Cook 10 oz fresh fusilli in a saucepan of boiling water according to the package directions, until "al dente," then drain and refresh under cold water. Meanwhile, steam 2 cups broccoli florets until just tender, then drain and refresh under cold water. Place the pasta and broccoli in a salad bowl and toss together with 1 cored, seeded, and sliced red bell pepper, 4 sliced scallions, 2 chopped plum tomatoes, and 8 oz white crab meat. Toss together with some Italian salad dressing and serve with crusty bread.

30 Crab Tart

Whisk together 4 eggs and ½ cup light cream in a bowl. Stir in 8 oz white crab meat, ½ diced red chile, 4 chopped scallions, 1 cored, seeded, and finely sliced red bell pepper, 1 tablespoon chopped parsley, and ¼ cup grated Parmesan. Pour the mixture into a 9 inch shop-bought pie crust and sprinkle with another ¼ cup grated Parmesan. Bake in a preheated oven, at 400°F, for 22–25 minutes.

 Tricolori Pita Pizzas

Serves 4

4 pita breads
1 tablespoon olive oil
1 (12 oz) package fresh spinach
¼ cup ketchup
2 yellow bell peppers, cored,
  seeded, and finely sliced
1 (7 oz) jar roasted red peppers,
  drained and sliced
2¼ cups shredded mozzarella
  cheese

- Cook the pita bread under a preheated hot broiler for 1–2 minutes. While they are still warm, run a knife down one side and slice them open to form 2 flat pieces of bread.

- Meanwhile, heat the olive oil in a skillet and add the spinach. Stir for 1–2 minutes, until it starts to wilt.

- Spread 1 tablespoon of the ketchup on each flatbread. Top with the spinach, sliced yellow and red peppers, and finally the mozzarella.

- Cook under a preheated hot broiler for 4–5 minutes, until the cheese is melted and golden.

2 Tricolori Pizzas

Using 2 medium store-bought pizza crusts, spread each with 2 tablespoons tomato puree. Top each one with 1 sliced tomato, ½ each of red and yellow bell peppers, seeded and sliced, ¼ thinly sliced red onion, and ½ cup shredded mozzarella cheese. Sprinkle with 6–8 shredded basil leaves and bake in a preheated oven, at 400°F, for 11–13 minutes. Cut into wedges and serve with a crisp green salad.

3 Tricolori Frittata

Heat 2 tablespoons olive oil in a flameproof skillet and cook 1 sliced red onion, 1 red bell pepper, and 1 yellow bell pepper, each cored, seeded, and sliced, and 2 crushed garlic cloves for 3–4 minutes, until tender, then add 1 (6 oz) package baby spinach leaves and stir until they are completely wilted. Beat together 7 eggs, 1 tablespoon milk, and some salt and pepper, then pour into the skillet. Stir the mixture around to make sure it all reaches the bottom of the skillet. Cook over low heat for 20 minutes, or until the bottom is set (use a spatula to pull away at the edges to check), then cook under a preheated hot broiler, until golden. Turn out onto a board and cut into wedges to serve.

Broccoli and Chili Orecchiette

Serves 4

5 cups broccoli florets
10 oz orecchiette
¼ cup olive oil
3 shallots, diced
4 garlic cloves, finely chopped
1 teaspoon dried red pepper flakes
2 tablespoons chopped parsley
2 tablespoons Parmesan cheese shavings, to serve

- Steam the broccoli for 4–5 minutes, until just tender. Drain.
- Cook the orecchiette in a saucepan of boiling water according to the package directions, until "al dente."
- Meanwhile, heat 2 tablespoons of the olive oil in a skillet and sauté the shallots with the garlic and red pepper flakes for 3–4 minutes.
- Add the broccoli to the skillet and stir to coat with the oil.
- Drain the pasta and add to the skillet with the remaining oil and chopped parsley. Toss together well.
- Serve sprinkled with Parmesan shavings.

 Broccoli and Tuna Pasta Casserole

Cook 8 oz fresh penne in a saucepan of boiling water according to the package directions, until "al dente." Meanwhile, steam 4 cups broccoli florets for 4–5 minutes, until just tender. Drain the penne and broccoli and mix together in an ovenproof dish with 4 diced tomatoes and a drained 12 oz can tuna. Pour over 1½ cups warmed store-bought cheese sauce and sprinkle with ¼ cup fresh bread crumbs and 2 tablespoons grated Parmesan cheese. Place under a preheated hot broiler for 3–4 minutes until golden. Serve with a crisp green salad.

 Broccoli and Bacon Pasta Salad

Halve, core, and seed 2 red bell peppers and cook, cut side down, under a preheated hot broiler for 6–7 minutes, until the skin turns black. Place in a bowl, cover with plastic wrap, and let stand until cool enough to handle. Meanwhile, cook 8 oz orecchiette in a saucepan of boiling water according to the package directions, until "al dente," then drain. Broil 8 bacon slices until crisp and then coarsely chop. Cut 2 heads of broccoli into florets and steam for 2–3 minutes, until just tender. Peel away the blackened skin from the peppers, then cut into strips. Quarter and seed 3 tomatoes, then cut into strips. For the dressing, whisk together ⅓ cup extra virgin olive oil, 2 tablespoons white wine vinegar, 2 teaspoons Dijon mustard, ½ crushed garlic clove, and 1 diced red chile in a small bowl, then season with salt and pepper. Toss together the pasta, vegetables, bacon, and 2 cups watercress in a large bowl, then pour the dressing over the salad to serve.

ITA-PIZZ-HUP

30 Spaghetti Bolognese with Grilled Cherry Tomatoes

Serves 4

1 tablespoon olive oil
2 bacon slices, chopped
1 large onion, chopped
2 garlic cloves, crushed
1 lb ground beef
⅔ cup red wine
1 (14½ oz) can diced tomatoes
½ teaspoon dried oregano
16 oz spaghetti
4 small vines of cherry tomatoes
¼ cup grated Parmesan cheese,
   to serve

- Heat the olive oil in a skillet and cook the bacon until golden. Add the onion and garlic and cook for 2–3 minutes, until the onion is softened.

- Increase the heat, add the ground beef, and cook to brown.

- Pour in the wine and boil until it has reduced in volume by half and then add the tomatoes and oregano. Simmer for 20–22 minutes.

- Meanwhile, cook the spaghetti in a saucepan of boiling water according to the package directions, until "al dente."

- Heat a ridged grill pan and cook the vine cherry tomatoes for 3–4 minutes.

- Drain the pasta and divide among 4 bowls. Spoon the Bolognese sauce over the pasta, top with a vine of cherry tomatoes, and serve sprinkled with grated Parmesan.

1 Spaghetti with Tomatoes

Cook 16 oz spaghetti in a saucepan of boiling water according to the package directions, until "al dente." Meanwhile, heat ¼ cup olive oil in a skillet and sauté 1 diced shallot, 1 crushed garlic clove, and 5 chopped plum tomatoes. Drain the pasta and toss with the tomatoes. Stir in 3 tablespoons chopped basil leaves and serve sprinkled with grated Parmesan cheese.

2 Tomato and Bolognese Pizza

Heat 1 tablespoon olive oil in a saucepan, add 1 chopped onion and 1 lb ground beef, and cook for 4–5 minutes, until browned. Stir in 1 cup store-bought tomato sauce and simmer for 3–4 minutes. Spoon the meat mixture over 4 store-bought small pizza crusts, top with 2 sliced tomatoes, sprinkle with ¼ cup shredded Mozzarella, and bake in a preheated oven, at 425°F, for 10–11 minutes, until the cheese is melted and golden.

ITA-PIZZ-PUD

30 Pea and Mint Risotto

Serves 4

1 tablespoon olive oil
2 shallots, finely diced
2 cups risotto rice
½ cup white wine
about 4 cups hot vegetable stock
⅔ cup fresh or frozen peas, defrosted
a small handful of mint leaves, chopped
3½ tablespoons butter
½ cup grated Parmesan cheese
salt and pepper

- Heat the olive oil in a large saucepan and sauté the shallots for 2–3 minutes, until softened but not browned.

- Stir in the rice and continue to stir, until the edges of the grains look translucent.

- Pour in the wine and cook for 1–2 minutes, until it is absorbed.

- Add a ladle of the hot vegetable stock and stir continuously, until it has all been absorbed.

- Repeat with the remaining hot stock, adding a ladle at a time, until the rice is "al dente."

- Stir in the peas, mint, butter, and half the Parmesan, season with salt and pepper, and cook for another 2–3 minutes.

- Serve sprinkled with the remaining grated Parmesan.

---

1 Pea and Mint Pasta Salad

Cook 8 oz fresh penne in a saucepan of boiling water according to the package directions, until "al dente," then drain and refresh under cold water. Meanwhile, cook 2 cups frozen peas in boiling water for 3–4 minutes, then drain and refresh under cold water. Toss the pasta and peas with 6 halved cherry tomatoes, 1 tablespoon chopped mint leaves, 1 cup chopped mozzarella cheese, and 4 pitted ripe black olives in a salad bowl. Add 1 (5 oz) package baby spinach leaves and 3–4 tablespoons Italian salad dressing and toss together gently.

2 Pea, Mint, and Rice Soup

Heat 2 tablespoons olive oil in a large saucepan and sauté 2 peeled and diced shallots and 1 diced celery stick for 4–5 minutes, until softened. Pour in 2½ cups vegetable stock, bring to a simmer, and add 2⅔ cups fresh or frozen peas. Cook for 10 minutes, or until the peas are tender. Add 2 tablespoons coarsely chopped mint leaves. Using a handheld blender, or in a food processor or blender, blend the soup until smooth. Stir in 1 cup store-bought prepared risotto of your choice, season to taste, and heat through until piping hot. Serve topped with a swirl of heavy cream or plain yogurt and 2 teaspoons chopped mint leaves.

Penne Arrabbiata

Serves 4

¼ cup olive oil
2 red chiles, finely sliced
2 garlic cloves, chopped
2½ cups canned diced tomatoes
6–8 basil leaves, shredded
16 oz penne
salt and pepper
¼ cup grated Parmesan cheese,
   to serve

- Heat the olive oil in a large skillet, add the red chiles and garlic, and cook for 2–3 minutes.

- Add the diced tomatoes and basil and simmer for 12 minutes. Season to taste.

- Meanwhile, cook the penne in a saucepan of boiling water according to the package directions, until "al dente." Drain the pasta and add it to the tomato sauce. Stir until combined.

- Serve sprinkled with grated Parmesan.

Quick Spicy Tomato Pasta

Heat 2 tablespoons olive oil in a large skillet and sauté 1 diced shallot and 1 finely diced red chile, until softened, then add 3–4 chopped plum tomatoes and 1 tablespoon chopped basil leaves. Meanwhile, cook 10 oz fresh conchiglie in a saucepan of boiling water according to the package directions, until "al dente," then drain. Remove the tomato mixture from the heat and stir in the pasta and 1 tablespoon balsamic vinegar. Place 2 cups watercress on a serving platter and spoon the tomato pasta over the greens. Serve sprinkled with 2 tablespoons shredded mozzarella cheese and 2 tablespoons toasted pine nuts.

Chili Tomato Tart

Roll out 1 sheet chilled, ready-to-bake puff pastry on a lightly floured work surface to 10 inches square. Place on a baking sheet and score a square about 1 inch in from the edge. Bake in a preheated oven, at 400°F, for 10 minutes, until golden. Slice 10 plum tomatoes (1¼ lb) and lay them on the center of the pastry. Sprinkle with ½ teaspoon dried red pepper flakes, 2 chopped pitted ripe black olives, and 1 tablespoon grated Parmesan. Bake for another 10–12 minutes and serve with steamed green beans and zucchini.

Fettucine with Dolcelatte and Spinach

Serves 4

16 oz fettucine

1 tablespoon olive oil

1 onion, chopped

2 garlic cloves, crushed

1¼ cups light cream

4 oz dolcelatte cheese

1 (5 oz) package baby spinach
leaves

salt and pepper

- Cook the fettucine in a saucepan of boiling water according to the package directions, until "al dente."

- Meanwhile, heat the olive oil in a skillet and sauté the onion and garlic for 4–5 minutes. Pour in the cream and simmer for 5–6 minutes, until the cream thickens a little.

- Stir in the dolcelatte and spinach and stir for 1 minute. Drain the pasta and add to the spinach. Season with salt and pepper then gently mix together and serve in warm bowls.

 Dolcelatte and Spinach Pizzas

Toast 4 whole wheat pita breads under a preheated hot broiler for 1–2 minutes on each side. Spread each one with 1 tablespoon ketchup. Meanwhile, heat 1 tablespoon olive oil in a skillet, add 1 (12 oz) package spinach leaves, and cook until wilted. Divide among the pita breads. Top each with ⅓ cup crumbled dolcelatte cheese, then sprinkle with 1 tablespoon pine nuts. Cook under a preheated broiler for 3–4 minutes, until the cheese is melted. Serve topped with a small handful of arugula leaves.

 Dolcelatte and Spinach Soup

Heat 1 tablespoon olive oil in a saucepan and sauté 1 chopped onion and 2 chopped garlic cloves for 3–4 minutes. Stir in 1 chopped potato and cook for another 1–2 minutes. Pour in 2 cups vegetable stock and bring to a boil. Simmer for 10 minutes and then stir in 2½ cups milk and bring to a simmer again. Add 1 (7 oz) package baby spinach leaves and the grated rind of 1 lemon and cook for 5–6 minutes, then stir in another 7 oz package baby spinach leaves and 2 oz dolcelatte. Using a handheld blender, or in a food processor or blender, blend the soup until smooth. Season and serve the soup with toasted pumpkin seeds and a few more crumbs of dolcelatte.

30 Saffron Risotto

Serves 4

2 tablespoons olive oil
1 onion, finely diced
1½ cups risotto rice
1 cup white wine
3 cups hot chicken stock
2 pinches of saffron strands
2 tablespoons butter
1½ cup grated Parmesan cheese

- Heat the olive oil in a saucepan and sauté the onion for 3–5 minutes, until softened.

- Stir in the rice and continue to stir, until the edges of the grains look translucent. Pour in the wine and cook for 1–2 minutes, until it is absorbed.

- Add a ladle of the hot chicken stock and the saffron and stir continuously, until it has all been absorbed. Repeat with the remaining hot stock, adding a ladle at a time, until the rice is "al dente."

- Remove from the heat and stir in the butter and half the grated Parmesan.

- Serve sprinkled with the remaining Parmesan.

 Warm Saffron Rice Salad

Heat 2 tablespoons olive oil in a skillet and cook 1 large chopped onion and 3 crushed garlic cloves for 4–5 minutes, until golden. Stir in 2 cups cooked long grain rice and heat through until piping hot. Meanwhile, crumble 1 large pinch of saffron threads into a small saucepan, add 3 tablespoons hot vegetable stock, and simmer for 1 minute, until infused, then stir into the rice with 2 tablespoons golden raisins, 3 tablespoons toasted slivered almonds, 2 tablespoons pitted green olives, 1 tablespoon chopped mint leaves, and 2 tablespoons chopped parsley.

 Saffron Scrambled Egg

Heat 1 cup milk in a saucepan with a large pinch of saffron threads. Cover and let stand for 4 minutes. Whisk together 8 extra-large eggs with some salt and pepper in a bowl and then add the saffron milk. Heat 2 tablespoons butter in a nonstick skillet and pour in the egg mixture. Let it sit without stirring for 20 seconds, then stir with a wooden spoon. Repeat this process, stirring and folding, until the egg is nearly cooked. Let stand for 2 minutes. Meanwhile, toast 8 slices of ciabatta on both sides. Spoon the egg over the toast to serve.

# Penne with Walnut Sauce

Serves 4

2 tablespoons olive oil

3 shallots, diced

1 cup walnut pieces

12 oz penne

2 tablespoons mascarpone cheese

3 tablespoons plain yogurt

2 tablespoons chopped parsley

pepper

¼ cup grated Parmesan cheese, to serve

- Heat the olive oil in a skillet and sauté the shallots for 2–3 minutes.

- Place half the walnuts in a food processor or blender and process until fine.

- Add the remaining walnuts to the skillet and cook for 5–6 minutes.

- Meahwhile, cook the penne in a saucepan of boiling water according to the package directions, until "al dente."

- Stir the ground walnuts, mascarpone, and yogurt into the skillet and stir until smooth. Stir in the chopped parsley and simmer gently for a few minutes.

- Drain the pasta, reserving 2 tablespoons of the cooking liquid. Add the pasta and liquid to the walnut sauce and toss together gently. Add pepper to taste.

- Serve sprinkled with grated Parmesan.

---

1 Walnut Penne Pesto Cook 16 oz penne according to the package directions, until "al dente." Meanwhile, Put 1½ cups walnut pieces and 1 crushed garlic clove in a food processor or blender and process until finely chopped. Add a handful of basil leaves, 1 cup grated Parmesan, 2 teaspoons lemon juice, and ¼ cup olive oil and process again until nearly smooth. Add a little more olive oil, if needed, to loosen the mixture. Drain the pasta and serve with the pesto.

3 Baked Tomato and Walnut Penne Cook 16 oz penne in a saucepan of boiling water according to the package directions, until "al dente." Meanwhile, heat 2 tablespoons olive oil in a saucepan and sauté 1 chopped onion, 2 chopped garlic cloves, and 1 teaspoon dried red pepper flakes for 2–3 minutes. Add 3½ lb skinned, seeded, and diced ripe tomatoes and ½ cup red wine and simmer for 6–8 minutes. Using a handheld blender, or in a food processor or blender, blend the tomato mixture to a chunky sauce and return to the pan. Stir in 3 teaspoons shredded basil leaves, 3 tablespoons chopped walnuts, and some salt and pepper. Drain the pasta and toss in the tomato sauce. Pour half the pasta into an ovenproof dish and sprinkle with 2 tablespoons grated Parmesan cheese and lay 4 oz sliced mozzarella cheese on top. Pour in the remaining pasta and repeat with the cheeses. Bake in a preheated oven, at 400°F, for 12–15 minutes. Serve with an arugula salad.

30 Tomato Risotto

Serves 4

1 tablespoon olive oil

1 onion, diced

2 garlic cloves, crushed

2 plum tomatoes

1 cup store-bought tomato sauce

1¼ cups hot vegetable stock

1 cup risotto rice

1 cup dried sun-dried tomatoes, cut into strips

2 tablespoons shredded basil leaves

salt and pepper

½ cup grated Parmesan cheese, to serve

- Heat the olive oil in a saucepan and sauté the onion and garlic for 5–6 minutes.

- Meanwhile, place the plum tomatoes in a large bowl and pour over boiling water. Let stand for 30 seconds, then drain and refresh under cold water. Peel off the skins, then seed and dice the tomatoes.

- Place the tomato sauce and stock in a small saucepan and bring to a simmer.

- Stir the rice into the onions and continue to stir, for 1–2 minutes until the edges of the grains look translucent.

- Add a ladle of the tomato sauce and stock and stir continuously, until it has all been absorbed.

- Repeat with the remaining hot stock, adding a ladle at a time, until the rice is "al dente."

- Stir in the diced tomatoes, sliced sun-dried tomatoes, and basil and season to taste.

- Serve sprinkled with grated Parmesan.

 Quick Tomato and Rice Salad

Skin and dice 4 plum tomatoes as above, and mix with 4 sliced scallions, 2½ cups cooked rice, 2 cups diced mozzarella cheese, and 2 tablespoons chopped basil leaves. Season and sprinkle with 2 tablespoons olive oil to serve.

 Tomato and Rice Soup

Heat 3 tablespoons olive oil in a large saucepan and sauté 1 chopped onion, 1 diced carrot, 1 celery stick, and 3 chopped garlic cloves for 3–4 minutes. Stir in ½ teaspoon fennel seeds, the grated rind of 1 orange, 2 tablespoons tomato paste, a 14½ oz can diced tomatoes, 1¼ cups vegetable stock, and ½ cup long grain rice. Season and simmer for 13–14 minutes, until the rice is cooked. Stir in 1 tablespoon shredded basil leaves to serve.

# Corn and Spinach Polenta

Serves 4

1 tablespoon olive oil, plus extra to serve

4 scallions, sliced

1¼ cups frozen corn kernels

3½ cups hot vegetable stock

1½ cups instant polenta

a large handful of spinach leaves

4 oz taleggio cheese, chopped

2 tablespoons grated Parmesan cheese

salt and pepper

- Heat the olive oil in a saucepan and sauté the scallions for 1 minute.

- Stir in the corn kernels, then pour in the vegetable stock and bring to a boil.

- Pour in the polenta and cook, stirring continuously, for 1 minute, until the polenta thickens.

- Stir in the spinach and cheese and season with salt and pepper. Serve drizzled with a little olive oil.

 Corn and Tuna Pasta Salad Cook 12 oz farfalle in a saucepan of boiling water according to the package directions, until "al dente." Drain, refresh under cold water, and place in a large bowl. Heat 2 tablespoons olive oil in a skillet and cook 2 (4 oz) tuna steaks for 2–3 minutes on each side. Let rest for 1–2 minutes, then break into chunks and add to the pasta with ½ cup sliced, drained roasted red peppers from a jar, ½ thickly sliced cucumber, 1 (11 oz) can corn kernels, drained, and 1 cup arugula leaves. Whisk together 3 tablespoons extra virgin olive oil, the juice of ½ lemon, ½ teaspoon whole-grain mustard, and 1 teaspoon honey in a small bowl, then toss with the salad and serve.

 Corn and Potato Soup Heat 2 tablespoons olive oil in a saucepan and sauté 1 chopped onion and 1 crushed garlic clove. Add 2 chopped potatoes and cook for another 3–4 minutes. Add 2½ cups frozen corn kernels and cook for 2 minutes, then pour in 5 cups vegetable stock. Bring to a boil and then simmer for 8–10 minutes, until the potato is tender. Stir in ½ cup heavy cream. Using a handheld blender, or in a food processor or blender, blend the soup until smooth. Season well and serve garnished with chopped chives.

Rigatoni with Mussels and Zucchini

Serves 4

3 lb mussels, cleaned
1 cup white wine
16 oz rigatoni
2 tablespoons olive oil
1 onion, diced
2 garlic cloves, crushed
2 zucchini, sliced

To serve

3 tablespoons grated Parmesan cheese
2 tablespoons chopped chives

- Place the mussels and wine in a large saucepan and cook over high heat for 5–6 minutes, until the mussels open. Drain, reserving the cooking liquid, and remove the mussels from their shells. Discard any mussels that have not opened.

- Cook the rigatoni in a saucepan of boiling water according to the package directions, until "al dente."

- Meanwhile, heat the olive oil in a saucepan and sauté the onion and garlic for 2–3 minutes, then add the zucchini and cook for another 4–5 minutes.

- Drain the pasta and stir into the zucchini with the mussels and strained mussel cooking liquid.

- Serve sprinkled with grated Parmesan and chopped chives.

Rigatoni, Mussel, and Feta Salad

Cook 12 oz rigatoni in a saucepan according to the package directions, until "al dente," adding 1 cup frozen peas 1 minute before the end of cooking. Meanwhile, mix together 1⅓ cups crumbled feta, with 2 cups arugula, the grated rind of 1 lemon, 1 shredded zucchini, 2 tablespoons chopped mint, and 20 smoked mussels. Drain the pasta and peas and refresh under cold water. Toss with the other ingredients and add 2 tablespoons extra virgin olive oil and the juice of ½ lemon. Season and serve.

Mussel and Zucchini Fritters

Coarsely chop 8 oz cooked mussels (smoked mussels can also be used). Put in a bowl, add 3 shredded zucchini, 4 sliced scallions, and 3 tablespoons chopped cilantro, and mix together. Sift 1 cup all-purpose flour into another bowl, then beat in ½ cup milk and 3 beaten eggs until you have a smooth batter. Stir in the mussel mixture. Heat 2 tablespoons olive oil in a skillet, pour in 1 tablespoon of the batter, and cook for 3–4 minutes on each side, until the fritter is golden brown. Mix together 1 cup plain yogurt and 2 tablespoons chopped mint leaves and serve with the fritters.

30 Cheese and Spinach Calzones

Serves 4

3⅔ cups white bread flour, plus extra for dusting
2¼ teaspoons active dry yeast
a pinch of salt
3 tablespoons olive oil
1¼ cups warm water
1 (12 oz) package fresh spinach
1⅔ cups ricotta cheese
¼ cup grated Parmesan cheese
¼ cup grated Pecorino cheese
4 scallions, sliced
1 teaspoon freshly ground black pepper

- To make the dough, place the flour, yeast, and salt in a large bowl and mix together. Make a well in the center. Stir in 1 tablespoon of the olive oil and most of the measured water. Mix together with your hand, gradually adding more water, if necessary, until you have a soft but not sticky dough.

- Turn the dough out onto a floured work surface and knead for 5–10 minutes, until the dough is smooth and elastic. Divide into 4 pieces and roll out to 8 inch circles.

- Heat the remaining olive oil in a skillet, add the spinach, and cook for 2–3 minutes, until completely wilted. Place in a bowl and stir in the remaining ingredients.

- Divide the mixture among the 4 circles of dough, placing the mixture onto one half of each circle, leaving a 1 inch clean edge. Brush the clean edges with water and then fold the other half over the filling and pinch together the edges to seal. Place the calzones on a baking sheet and bake in a preheated oven, at 425°F, for 6–8 minutes, until the dough is cooked and the filling is hot.

 Cheese and Spinach Stuffed Pita Breads

Heat 1 tablespoon olive oil in a skillet and sauté 1 sliced red onion for a few minutes, then add 1 (6 oz) package spinach leaves and stir to wilt. Remove from the heat and mix with ¼ cup grated Parmesan and 8 oz torn mozzarella. Heat 4 pita breads, slice along one side, and open up. Fill each pita with the spinach filling and top with slices of salami.

 Cheese and Spinach Pasta

Salad Toast ¾ cup pine nuts in a dry skillet, until golden. Cook 16 oz fusilli in a saucepan of boiling water according to the package directions, until "al dente." Drain and refresh the pasta under cold running water and then toss with 2 tablespoons olive oil to prevent the pasta from sticking together. In a serving bowl, toss together 1 (5 oz) package baby spinach leaves with 2 cups shredded cheddar cheese and ¼ cup grated Parmesan cheese. Stir in 4 sliced scallions, 6 halved cherry tomatoes, and the pasta. Whisk together 2 tablespoons olive oil and 1 tablespoon balsamic vinegar, then pour the dressing over the salad. Serve sprinkled with the toasted pine nuts.

20 Spaghetti Puttanesca

Serves 4

1 tablespoon olive oil

4 garlic cloves, thinly sliced

2 (14½ oz) cans diced tomatoes

2 tablespoons capers, chopped

4 anchovy fillets, chopped

a handful of green olives, pitted
  and sliced

1 teaspoon dried red pepper
  flakes

a small handful of parsley,
  coarsely chopped

16 oz spaghetti

- Heat the olive oil in a saucepan and cook the garlic for 1 minute, then add the tomatoes, capers, anchovies, olives, and red pepper flakes. Simmer for 10 minutes, until the sauce starts to thicken. Stir in the chopped parsley.

- Meanwhile, cook the spaghetti in a saucepan of boiling water according to the package directions, until "al dente." Drain the pasta, toss in the sauce, and serve.

10 Quick Green Bean and Anchovy

Risotto Steam 4 cups trimmed green beans for 6–7 minutes, until just tender. Meanwhile, boil 4 eggs for 4 minutes, then refresh under cold running water. Remove the shells. Whisk together 3 tablespoons extra virgin olive oil, 1 tablespoon sherry vinegar, 1 teaspoon Dijon mustard, and a pinch of sugar in a small bowl. Heat a 13 oz package of cooked risotto of your choice according to the package directions until piping hot, then spoon onto 4 warm plates or bowls. Divide the beans among the plates, then top each with a halved soft-boiled egg and 2–3 halved anchovy fillets. Drizzle with the dressing and serve.

30 Sicilian Anchovy Spaghetti

Halve 6 plum tomatoes, put in a roasting pan, and roast for 15 minutes in a preheated oven, at 400°F. Cook 12 oz spaghetti in a saucepan of boiling water according to the package directions, until "al dente." Meanwhile, heat 1 tablespoon olive oil in a skillet and cook 3 eggs until the white is set but the yolk is still runny. Dice the tomatoes coarsely and stir in 4 chopped anchovy fillets, 1 chopped garlic clove, 1 tablespoon chopped pickles, and 1 cup fresh bread crumbs. Chop the eggs and add to the mixture. Drain the pasta and stir into the sauce with 1 tablespoon olive oil and 1 tablespoon chopped parsley. Serve immediately sprinkled with 2 tablespoons grated Parmesan cheese.

30 Eggplant and Zucchini Ratatouille Pizzas

Serves 4

2 tablespoons olive oil
1 red onion, chopped
2 garlic cloves, crushed
1 large eggplant, cut into
  bite-size pieces
3 zucchini, halved and sliced
1 red bell pepper, cored, seeded,
  and chopped
1 yellow bell pepper, cored,
  seeded, and chopped
1 (14½ oz) can diced tomatoes
4 individual store-bought
  pizza crusts
a small handful of basil leaves,
  torn
2 cups shredded mozzarella
  cheese

- Heat the olive oil in a large skillet and sauté the onion and garlic for 1–2 minutes. Add the eggplant and cook for 3–4 minutes, then add the zucchini and bell peppers, and cook over low heat for 4–5 minutes.

- Stir in the diced tomatoes, bring to a simmer, and cook for 2–3 minutes, until the vegetables start to soften.

- Using a slotted spoon, divide the mixture among the pizza crusts on 2 baking sheets. Top with the basil and shredded mozzarella and bake in a preheated oven, at 425°F, for 11–13 minutes. Serve immediately.

---

10 Quick Eggplant and Zucchini Pizzas

Toast 4 whole wheat pita breads under a preheated hot broiler for 1–2 minutes on each side. Spread each one with 1 tablespoon ketchup. Top each with 1–2 pieces of store-bought chargrilled eggplant, 1–2 pieces of roasted red pepper from a jar, 1 slice of store-bought chargrilled zucchini, and 1 tablespoon shredded mozzarella cheese. Cook under a preheated hot broiler for 3–4 minutes, until the cheese is melted.

20 Rice, Zucchini, and Feta Salad

Cook 1 cup long-grain rice in a saucepan of boiling water according to the package directions, until tender, then drain and refresh under cold water. Slice 2 zucchini thinly with a vegetable peeler. Toss together the rice, zucchini, 4 sliced scallions, 1 finely diced red chile, 2 tablespoons chopped, drained marinated eggplant, 1⅓ cups crumbled feta cheese, and 2 tablespoons chopped parsley. Drizzle with

2 tablespoons olive oil and 1 tablespoon white wine vinegar and gently toss together.

Creamy Mushroom and Cabbage Polenta

Serves 4

1 small savoy cabbage, shredded

1 tablespoon olive oil

4 oz pancetta or bacon, diced

2 shallots, diced

2 garlic cloves, crushed

2 cups sliced cremini mushrooms

1¾ cups water

1¾ cups milk

1¼ cups instant polenta

2 tablespoons butter

2 teaspoons chopped thyme leaves

⅔ cup crumbled Gorgonzola or other blue cheese

- Steam the cabbage for 4–5 minutes and then keep warm.

- Heat the olive oil in a saucepan and cook the diced pancetta for 2–3 minutes. Add the shallots and garlic and cook for another 3–4 minutes.

- Stir in the mushrooms and continue to cook for 5–6 minutes.

- Meanwhile, bring the measured water and milk to a boil in another saucepan. Pour in the polenta and cook, stirring continuously, for 1 minute, until thick and creamy. Stir in the butter and thyme.

- Stir the steamed cabbage and Gorgonzola into the mushroom mixture, until the cheese starts to melt.

- Divide the soft polenta among 4 plates and spoon the mushroom and cabbage mixture over it to serve.

Quick Mushroom Polenta

Heat 2 tablespoons olive oil in a saucepan and sauté 1 diced onion, 2 crushed garlic cloves, and ¼ teaspoon dried red pepper flakes for 2–3 minutes. Add 1 cup chopped cremini mushrooms and cook for 2–3 minutes. Pour in 3½ cups boiling water and then 1¼ cups instant polenta. Cook for 1–2 minutes, stirring continuously. Stir in 3 tablespoons grated Parmesan cheese and serve drizzled with a little olive oil.

Cabbage, Mushroom, and Mozzarella Casserole

Cut a cabbage into quarters and place in a casserole dish. Sprinkle with 1 chopped apple, 1 chopped onion, 2 cups sliced cremini mushrooms, 2 tablespoons chopped parsley, and 2 cups shredded mozzarella. Pour 1 cup hot vegetable stock and 2 tablespoons white wine over the vegetables. Cover and bake in a preheated oven, at 400°F, for 22–25 minutes, until the cabbage is tender.

ITA-PIZZ-ZOB

 # Fusilli with Watercress, Raisins and Pine Nuts

Serves 4

16 oz fusilli
2 tablespoons olive oil
8 oz watercress or arugula, coarsely chopped
⅓ cup raisins
½ cup toasted pine nuts
grated rind of 1 lemon
Parmesan cheese shavings, to serve

- Cook the fusilli in a saucepan of boiling water according to the package directions, until "al dente."

- Meanwhile, heat the olive oil in a large saucepan and add the watercress. Stir until wilted and then add the raisins.

- Drain the pasta and add to the watercress and raisins. Add the pine nuts and lemon rind, then toss together.

- Serve sprinkled with Parmesan shavings.

 ## Fusilli and Watercress Salad

Cook 12 oz fusilli in a saucepan of boiling water according to the package directions, until "al dente." Drain and refresh under cold water. Mix together the pasta with 2 carrots, 2 zucchini, and 1 cored and seeded red bell pepper, which have all been cut into matchsticks. Add 3 oz watercress or arugula. Whisk together 3 tablespoons extra virgin olive oil, 1 tablespoon sherry vinegar, 1 crushed garlic clove, ½ teaspoon mustard, and ½ teaspoon honey. Drizzle the dressing over the salad and serve sprinkled with 2 tablespoons toasted pine nuts.

 ## Watercress and Potato Soup

Heat 2 tablespoons olive oil in a large saucepan and sauté 2 sliced leeks, 2 chopped potatoes, and 3 cups chopped watercress. Cover and sauté over low heat for 10 minutes, stirring halfway through. Pour in 3¾ cups vegetable stock and simmer for 10–15 minutes, until the potatoes are tender. Using a handheld blender, or in a food processor or blender, blend the soup until smooth. Return to the pan, stir in 3 tablespoons crème fraîche or sour cream and salt and pepper, and bring back to a simmer. Serve with another swirl of crème fraîche or sour cream and garnish with a sprig of watercress.

ITA-PIZZ-BEF

30 Pepperoni Pasta

Serves 4

16 oz spiral pasta
1 tablespoon olive oil
1 onion, chopped
2 red bell peppers, cored, seeded, and chopped
1 lb ground beef
1 (14½ oz) can diced tomatoes
½ cup red wine
4 oz pepperoni sausage, sliced
¼ cup grated Parmesan cheese

- Cook the spiral pasta in a saucepan of boiling water according to the package directions, until "al dente."

- Meanwhile, heat the olive oil in a skillet and sauté the onion and red bell pepper for 4–5 minutes. Stir in the ground beef and brown for 3–4 minutes.

- Pour in the diced tomatoes, red wine, and pepperoni, bring to a boil, and simmer for 8–10 minutes.

- Drain the pasta and stir into the meat mixture. Pour into an ovenproof dish and sprinkle with the grated Parmesan.

- Cook under a preheated hot broiler for 2–3 minutes, until the cheese is golden. Serve immediately.

1 Pepperoni Rice Salad

Heat 2 tablespoons olive oil in a skillet and sauté 1 chopped onion for a few minutes, then stir in 5 oz chopped pepperoni sausage and cook until a little crisp around the edges. Stir in 2 cups cooked rice, 2 tablespoons chopped sun-dried tomatoes, and 1 cup defrosted frozen peas. Serve sprinkled with chopped parsley.

2 Pepperoni Pizza

Place 4 store-bought, individual pizza crusts onto 2 baking sheets and spread each one with ⅓ cup tomato puree. Top each one with 1 sliced tomato, 3 oz sliced pepperoni, and ½ cup shredded mozzarella cheese. Bake in a preheated oven, at 425°F, for 11–13 minutes, until the cheese is melted and golden.

30 Cheese Gnocchi with Spinach and Walnuts

Serves 4

1 tablespoon olive oil
8 oz baby spinach leaves
1 lb store-bought gnocchi
1 cup crème fraîche or sour cream
½ teaspoon whole=grain mustard
⅔ cup shredded cheddar cheese
¼ cup grated Pecorino cheese
¼ cup walnut pieces

- Heat the olive oil in a skillet and cook the spinach until it has wilted.

- Cook the gnocchi in a saucepan of boiling water according to the package directions. Drain.

- Place the crème fraîche and mustard in a saucepan, stir in about half of each of the cheeses, and cook for 2–3 minutes, then stir in the spinach and gnocchi to heat through. Stir in the walnuts.

- Pour into an ovenproof dish and sprinkle with the remaining cheese. Cook under a preheated hot broiler for 3–4 minutes, until golden and serve.

---

10 Cheese and Spinach Omelet

Whisk together 12 eggs in a bowl and season well. Heat 1 tablespoon butter and ½ tablespoon olive oil in an omelet pan or small skillet and pour in one-quarter of the egg mixture. Move it around for 1 minute to let all the egg start cooking. When cooked underneath, sprinkle the omelet with a small handful of baby spinach leaves and ½ cup shredded Fontina or cheddar cheese. Cook for 1–2 minutes then, using a spatula, fold one half of the omelet over the other and slide onto a warm plate to serve. Repeat 3 more times with the remaining egg mixture and the same amount of spinach and cheese to make 4 omelets.

20 Cheesy Spinach Polenta with Creamy Mushrooms

Heat 2 tablespoons olive oil in a saucepan and sauté 3 cups chopped cremini mushrooms with 2 chopped shallots and 2 chopped garlic cloves. Stir in 3 tablespoons crème fraîche or sour cream with ½ teaspoon whole-grain mustard and ¼ cup chopped toasted walnuts. Heat 5½ cups boiling vegetable stock in another saucepan, pour in 1½ cups instant polenta, and cook, stirring continuously, for 5–6 minutes, until thick and creamy. Remove from the heat and stir in 1 cup shredded Fontina or cheddar cheese and 2 cups coarsely chopped fresh baby spinach leaves. Divide the polenta among 4 warm bowls, spoon the creamy mushrooms over the polenta, and serve sprinkled with 2 tablespoons grated Pecorino cheese.

ITA-PIZZ-HEC

30 Margherita Pizza

Serves 4

7⅓ cups white bread flour,
  plus extra for dusting
1½ tablespoons active dry yeast
a pinch of salt
2 tablespoons olive oil
2½ cups warm water
2 cups tomato puree
6 plum tomatoes, sliced
1 lb mozzarella, sliced

- To make the dough, place the flour, yeast, and salt in a large bowl and mix together. Make a well in the center. Stir in 1 tablespoon of the olive oil and most of the measured water.

- Mix together with your hand, gradually adding more water, if necessary, until you have a soft but not sticky dough.

- Turn the dough out onto a floured work surface and knead for 5–10 minutes, until the dough is smooth and elastic.

- Divide into 4 pieces and roll out to 12 inch circles, then place on pizza pans or baking sheets.

- Spread each one with tomato puree, then cover with slices of tomato and mozzarella.

- Bake in a preheated oven, at 425°F, for 6–7 minutes, until the cheese is melted and golden. Serve immediately.

 Super Speedy Tomato Pizzas

Toast 4 pita breads on both sides under a preheated hot broiler. Spread each with 1 tablespoon ketchup, then cover with 4 sliced tomatoes. Top each one with ⅔ cup shredded or 3 oz sliced mozzarella and cook under the hot broiler until the cheese is melted and golden. Serve sprinkled with chopped basil.

 Spinach and Tomato Baked

Eggs Steam 1 (12 oz) package spinach until wilted and drain well. Heat 1 tablespoon olive oil in a skillet and cook 3 diced tomatoes for 3–4 minutes. Stir in 2 tablespoons chopped basil leaves and season well. Add the wilted spinach and cook for 1–2 minutes. Divide the mixture among 4 ramekin dishes and then break an egg into each one. Add a pat of butter to each dish and bake in a preheated oven, at 375°F, for 10–12 minutes. Serve with toasted ciabatta.

ITA-PIZZ-RIZ

Pea and Scallion Linguine

Serves 4

⅓ cup olive oil
2 garlic cloves, chopped
a large handful of mint leaves
⅓ cup toasted pine nuts
½ cup grated Parmesan cheese
12 oz linguine
1½ cups fresh or frozen peas
4 scallions, sliced

- Place the olive oil, garlic, mint, pine nuts, and grated Parmesan in a blender or food processor and blend until smooth.

- Cook the linguini in a saucepan of boiling water according to the package directions, until "al dente."

- Meanwhile, cook the peas in a saucepan of boiling water for 3–4 minutes and then drain.

- Drain the pasta. Return to the pan and gently stir in the mint pesto, peas, and scallions. Serve immediately.

10 Spaghetti with Pea and Mint Pesto

Cook 16 oz thin spaghetti according to the package directions, until "al dente." Meanwhile, blanch 1¾ cups frozen peas in a saucepan of boiling water for 2 minutes, then drain and refresh under cold water. Place the peas in a food processor with 2 crushed garlic cloves, ⅓ cup toasted pine nuts, ½ cup grated Parmesan cheese, ⅓ cup extra virgin olive oil, a small handful of mint leaves, and some salt and pepper. Pulse briefly until coarsely chopped but not smooth. Drain the spaghetti, then return to the pan with the pesto and toss together well. Serve sprinkled with Parmesan cheese shavings.

30 Pea and Mint Tart

Cook 4 oz diced pancetta in a dry skillet until crisp. Add 2 finely chopped shallots and cook for another 2–3 minutes. Spoon the mixture into the bottom of a 9 inch store-bought pie crust. Beat together 4 extra-large eggs and 1¼ cups heavy cream in a small bowl. Stir in 1½ cups defrosted frozen peas, 2 tablespoons chopped mint leaves, and ½ cup shredded Gruyére or Swiss cheese. Pour the mixture into the pie crust, sprinkle with 2 tablespoons grated Parmesan cheese, and cook in a preheated oven, at 400°F, for 20–22 minutes, until golden. Serve warm or cold with salad.

ITA-PIZZ-FYR

QuickCook
Fish and Seafood

Recipes listed by cooking time

30

20

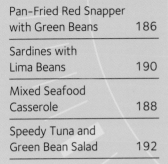

10

Herb Butter Squid

Serves 4

1 stick butter

grated rind of 1 lime and juice
  of ½ lime

2 tablespoons chopped mint
  leaves

2 tablespoons chopped basil
  leaves

1 tablespoon olive oil

1 lb squid rings

- Mix together the butter, lime rind, mint, and basil in a small bowl. Stir in the lime juice.

- Heat the olive oil in a large skillet and cook the squid rings for 1–2 minutes on each side. Remove the squid from the skillet and place them in a hot dish.

- Dab the squid with the herb butter and lightly toss together. Serve immediately.

 Spiced Squid with Chickpeas

Place 1 lb squid, cleaned and cut into rings, in a nonmetallic bowl and toss in the juice of 1 lime, 1 finely diced red chile, and 8 shredded basil leaves. Let marinate for 10 minutes. Place 1 shredded romaine lettuce and 8 halved cherry tomatoes in a large salad bowl. Heat 2 tablespoons olive oil in a skillet and sauté 1 thinly sliced red onion for 3–4 minutes. Add the squid and marinade and cook over high heat for 2–3 minutes. Add 1 (15 oz) can chickpeas (garbanzo beans), drained, and stir to coat with the spicy oil. Pour everything over the salad greens and gently toss together.

Crispy Squid

Place 1⅔ cups all-purpose flour, 1 tablespoon pepper, and a pinch each of salt and chili powder into a freezer bag. Shake everything together and then add 1 lb squid rings. Pour peanut oil into a deep-fryer or large saucepan and heat to 350–375°F or until a cube of bread browns in 30 seconds when dropped into the oil. Remove some of the squid from the flour and shake off the excess. Working in batches, gently drop into the hot oil and cook for 3–4 minutes, until crisp. Remove with a slotted spoon and drain on paper towels. Meanwhile, stir 2 crushed garlic cloves into ⅓ cup mayonnaise in a bowl. Serve the squid with the garlic mayonnaise and wedges of lemon.

Grilled Swordfish with Salsa Verde

Serves 4

1½ teaspoons Dijon mustard

2 cups extra virgin olive oil

4 anchovy fillets, chopped

a handful each of parsley, basil, mint, and tarragon

2 tablespoons capers

1 garlic clove, crushed

2 tablespoons olive oil

4 swordfish steaks, about 5 oz each

juice of 1 lemon

salt and pepper

crisp green salad, to serve

- Whisk together the mustard and 1 cup of the extra virgin olive oil in a bowl until they have emulsified. Stir in the anchovies.

- Chop together the herbs and capers and add them to the oil mixture along with the crushed garlic. Gradually add more of the extra virgin olive oil until the sauce has a spooning consistency.

- Heat a ridged grill pan until hot. Brush the swordfish steaks on both sides with the olive oil and season well. Grill the steaks for 2–3 minutes on each side, or until cooked through but still very moist.

- Add the lemon juice to the salsa verde and serve spooned over the grilled fish with a crisp green salad.

 Swordfish with Quick Salsa Verde

Cook 4 (5 oz) swordfish steaks under a preheated hot broiler for 2–3 minutes on each side, until cooked through. Meanwhile, place 2 garlic cloves, a small handful of capers, a small handful of pickles, 4 anchovy fillets, 2 large handfuls of parsley, a handful of basil leaves, a handful of mint leaves, 1 tablespoon mustard, 3 tablespoons white wine vinegar, ½ cup extra virgin olive oil, and some salt and pepper in a food processor or blender. Blend until fully mixed and serve with the swordfish.

 Swordfish with a Smoky Tomato

Sauce Whisk together 3 tablespoons extra virgin olive oil, the juice of 1 lemon, leaves from 3 thyme sprigs, and 2 teaspoons pepper in a bowl. Put 4 swordfish steaks in a shallow dish large enough for them to sit side by side. Pour the marinade over the fish and let stand for 20 minutes. Meanwhile, cut 12 tomatoes in half and place, cut side up, on a baking sheet. Sprinkle with 1 teaspoon smoked paprika and 2 tablespoons olive oil, and season well. Sprinkle with a small handful of thyme leaves.

Cook under a preheated hot broiler until the skins have blackened a little. Spoon the tomatoes and juices into a saucepan over gentle heat. Add a small handful of basil leaves and lightly crush the tomatoes with the leaves. Add 1 tablespoon red wine vinegar, 1 teaspoon dark brown sugar, and ½ cup pitted black olives. Wilt 1 (7 oz) package baby spinach leaves in a separate saucepan and drain well. Heat a ridged grill pan and cook the marinated swordfish for 2–3 minutes on each side. Serve on a bed of wilted spinach, with the smoky tomato sauce.

30 Stuffed Mussels

Serves 4

2–3 lb large mussels, cleaned
  (about 48 mussels)
1⅓ cups bread crumbs
½ cup walnut pieces
1¾ sticks butter
6 garlic cloves, chopped
juice of 1 lemon
2 tablespoons grated
  Parmesan cheese
2 tablespoons chopped tarragon
a small handful of parsley,
  chopped

- Steam the mussels in a large, covered saucepan until they open, then drain. Discard any mussels that do not open. Break off the empty half of the shells and place the mussels on a baking sheet.

- Place the bread crumbs, walnuts, butter, garlic, lemon juice, and grated Parmesan in a food processor and process until the mixture starts to come together. Add the herbs and blend until combined.

- Divide the herb mixture among the mussels, making sure each mussel is covered. Cook under a preheated hot broiler for 2–3 minutes, until the stuffing is golden. You may need to cook the mussels in batches if you cannot fit them all on 1 baking sheet.

- Serve immediately.

 Smoked Mussel Bruschetta

Toast 8 slices of ciabatta on both sides, then rub each slice with a garlic clove. Coarsely chop 7 oz smoked mussels and mix with 2 coarsely diced tomatoes, 1 tablespoon chopped parsley, and the juice of ½ lemon. Spoon the mussel mixture onto the toast and serve topped with a few arugula leaves.

 Mussel and Tomato Linguine

Steam 2 lb cleaned mussels over ¼ cup white wine in a large saucepan until they have opened. Drain the mussels, reserving the cooking liquid, discarding any that do not open. Heat ¼ cup olive oil in a saucepan and sauté 1 finely chopped onion, 4 sliced garlic cloves, and ¼ teaspoon dried red pepper flakes. Add 3 cups halved cherry tomatoes and cook for 5 minutes. Meanwhile, cook 1 lb linguine in a saucepan of boiling water according to the package directions, until "al dente." Strain the mussel cooking liquid into the pan of tomatoes and add the mussels, 2 tablespoons chopped parsley, and the drained linguine. Toss everything together, season and serve.

3⃝ Mackerel with Beet and Potato Salad

Serves 4

8 oz small new potatoes
2 tablespoons olive oil
4 scallions, sliced
4 small, cooked beets, thickly
sliced
4 mackerel fillets
grated rind and juice of 1 lemon
½ teaspoon freshly ground
black pepper
2 cups watercress or arugula
2 tablespoons capers, coarsely
chopped
⅔ cup plain yogurt
4 lemon wedges, to serve

- Cook the new potatoes in a saucepan of boiling water, until tender.

- Drain and toss the potatoes with the olive oil, scallions, and beets in a large bowl.

- Place the mackerel fillets, skin side down, on a baking sheet, squeeze the lemon juice over the fish, and season with the pepper. Cook under a preheated hot broiler for 3–4 minutes on each side, until cooked through.

- Meanwhile, toss the watercress into the potato salad, and stir the capers and lemon rind into the yogurt in a small bowl.

- Divide the salad among 4 plates and top each with 1 broiled mackerel fillet and a spoonful of yogurt dressing. Serve with lemon wedges.

1⃝ Smoked Mackerel and Beet Pâté

Mix together 10 oz skinned and flaked smoked mackerel, the juice of ½ lemon, ⅔ cup cream cheese, 2 teaspoons horseradish sauce, and some salt and pepper. Serve the pâté on slices of toasted ciabatta and top with grated cooked fresh beets.

2⃝ Smoked Mackerel and Beet Risotto

Put 2 small cooked fresh beets in a food processor or blender and blend until smooth. Heat 1 tablespoon olive oil in a large skillet and sauté 2 diced shallots for 2–3 minutes, until softened but not browned. Stir in 2 cups risotto rice and continue to stir, until the edges of the grains look translucent. Pour in ½ cup white wine and cook for 1–2 minutes, until it is absorbed. Add a ladle from 3¾ cups hot vegetable stock and stir continuously, until it has all been absorbed. Repeat with the remaining stock, adding a ladle at a time, until the rice is "al dente." Stir in the beet puree, another 2 diced, cooked beets, and 2 flaked smoked mackerel fillets. Serve sprinkled with chopped chives.

3 Italian Fish and Seafood Stew

Serves 4

3 tablespoons olive oil
1 onion, finely chopped
1 fennel bulb, finely chopped
2 garlic cloves, sliced
1 teaspoon fennel seeds
1 (14½ oz) can diced tomatoes
8 oz clams, cleaned
9 cups fish stock
a pinch of saffron threads
8 oz cooked jumbo shrimp
4 (4 oz) red snapper fillets
1 lb monkfish fillet, cut
  into chunks
2 tablespoons chopped parsley,

- Heat 2 tablespoons of the olive oil in a large saucepan and sauté the onion, fennel, garlic, and fennel seeds for 4–5 minutes.

- Stir in the diced tomatoes and cook everything for another 12–14 minutes, until the vegetables are tender.

- Meanwhile, heat the remaining olive oil in a saucepan and cook the clams, covered, for 2–3 minutes, until they have all opened. Discard any clams that do not open.

- Pour the stock and saffron into the tomato mixture and bring to a boil. Add the shrimp, red snapper, and monkfish and simmer for 5–6 minutes, until the fish is cooked through and the shrimp turn pink. Add the cooked clams.

- Stir through the chopped parsley and serve immediately.

---

1 Seafood Salad

Whisk together 3 tablespoons extra virgin olive oil, the juice of ½ lemon, 1 crushed garlic clove, and 2 tablespoons chopped parsley. Toss together 10 oz chilled, cooked mixed seafood with 1 thinly sliced fennel bulb and 12 halved cherry tomatoes. Trim 2 endive heads and divide the leaves among 4 plates. Toss together the seafood and dressing and spoon on top of the endive leaves. Serve with warm ciabatta.

2 Seafood Pasta

Cook 12 oz spaghetti in a saucepan of boiling water according to the package directions, until "al dente." Meanwhile, heat 1 tablespoon olive oil in a skillet and sauté 1 chopped onion and 2 crushed garlic cloves for 2–3 minutes. Stir in 1 teaspoon smoked paprika, 1 (14½ oz) can diced tomatoes, and ½ cup vegetable stock. Bring to a simmer, add 8 oz chilled, cooked mixed seafood, and cook for 3–4 minutes. Drain the pasta and add to the seafood sauce with 2 tablespoons chopped parsley. Serve immediately.

 # Tuna in Tomato and Caper Sauce

Serves 4

¼ cup olive oil

1¼ lb fresh tuna, cut into
 bite-size pieces

1 large onion, sliced

3 red bell peppers, cored, seeded,
 and sliced into rings

8 capers

½ cup white wine

1 (14½ oz) can diced tomatoes

½ cup water

2 tablespoons chopped basil
 leaves

8 slices of ciabatta

lemon wedges, to serve

- Heat 2 tablespoons of the olive oil in a large skillet and brown the tuna on all sides.

- Add the onion, red bell peppers, capers, and white wine. Simmer to reduce the wine by half and then pour in the diced tomatoes and measured water. Simmer for 10–12 minutes. Stir in the basil.

- Toast the ciabatta on both sides, then place 2 slices on 4 plates and spoon the tuna and sauce over the toasts. Serve with lemon wedges.

 Tuna and Caper Spaghetti

Cook 16 oz spaghetti in a saucepan of boiling water according to the package directions, until "al dente." Meanwhile, mix together 1 finely diced red onion, 1 finely chopped red chile, 2 crushed garlic cloves, 2 tablespoons capers, the juice of 1 lemon, 3 tablespoons olive oil, 2 tablespoons chopped parsley, and 1 (5 oz) oz can tuna, drained and flaked. Drain the pasta and toss everything together to serve.

 Tuna Rice Salad

Cook 1 cup long-grain rice in a saucepan of boiling water according to the package directions, until tender. Drain and refresh under cold water, then place in a large bowl. Stir in 1 (5 oz) can tuna, drained and flaked, ⅔ cup defrosted and blanched peas, 2 cored, seeded, and diced red bell peppers, 1 cored, seeded, and diced yellow bell pepper, 3 diced tomatoes, 4 sliced scallions, 2 tablespoons chopped parsley, and ½ cup sliced green olives. Sprinkle with the juice of 1 lemon and 3 tablespoons extra virgin olive oil, season, and mix well to serve.

 # Shrimp and Cannellini Bean Salad

Serves 4

4 plum tomatoes
2 tablespoons olive oil
4 scallions
1 red chile, seeded and sliced
2 garlic cloves, sliced
6–8 basil leaves, shredded
1 tablespoon balsamic vinegar
1 teaspoon superfine or
  granulated sugar
1 (15 oz) can cannellini beans,
  rinsed and drained
8 oz cooked peeled jumbo shrimp
1 tablespoon chopped parsley
1 romaine lettuce
salt and pepper

- Place the tomatoes in a bowl and pour over boiling water. Let stand for 1 minute, then drain and refresh under cold water. Peel off the skins and dice the tomatoes. Place in a large bowl.

- Heat the olive oil in a skillet and sauté the scallions, red chile, and garlic for 2–3 minutes. Turn off the heat and stir in the basil, letting it wilt in the remaining heat.

- Add the balsamic vinegar and sugar and stir until the sugar has dissolved. Season.

- Add the drained cannellini beans, shrimp, and chopped parsley to the diced tomatoes, then pour the dressing over the salad and toss together.

- Place a few romaine lettuce leaves on 4 plates, then spoon the salad on top.

10 Cannellini Beans with Tuna

Heat 3 tablespoons olive oil in a large skillet and sauté 1 finely diced red onion and 2 crushed garlic cloves, until softened. Stir in 1 (15 oz) can cannellini beans, rinsed and drained. Cook for 2–3 minutes to infuse the flavors, then remove from the heat and stir in ¼ cup chopped parsley and 1 (5 oz) can tuna, drained and flaked. Season with salt and pepper and serve.

30 Shrimp Kebabs and Garlic and Cannellini Beans

Mix together 2 teaspoons honey, the juice of 1 lime, and 1 crushed garlic clove in a bowl. Pour the marinade over 12 oz cooked, peeled jumbo shrimp and let marinate for 5 minutes. Remove the stems from 1½ cups small button mushrooms. Core and seed 1 red bell pepper and chop it into medium chunks and slice 1 zucchini. Remove the shrimp from the marinade and thread them onto skewers, alternating with the vegetables. Place the kebabs under a preheated hot broiler or on a hot ridged grill pan and cook for 6–7 minutes, until the edges of the vegetables start to turn golden, brushing the shrimp with the remaining marinade every few minutes. Meanwhile, make the 10-minute recipe on the left, omitting the tuna, and serve with the kebabs once cooked, or stuff the salad into pita breads with shredded lettuce to accompany the kebabs.

30 Chili Cod in Tomato Sauce

Serves 4

2 tablespoons olive oil

1 onion, diced

2 garlic cloves, crushed

¼ teaspoon dried
   red pepper flakes

1 red bell pepper, cored, seeded,
   and thinly sliced

1 (14½ oz) can diced tomatoes

½ cup white wine

12 ripe black olives, pitted
   and sliced

4 skinless cod loin fillets, about
   5 oz each

steamed green beans, to serve
   (optional)

- Heat the olive oil in a large skillet and sauté the onion, garlic, and red pepper flakes for 3–4 minutes. Add the red bell pepper and cook for another 3–4 minutes.

- Pour in the diced tomatoes, white wine, and black olives and simmer for 8 minutes.

- Add the cod loin fillets to the skillet and cook for 8–10 minutes, turning once if not covered by the liquid, until cooked through.

- Serve with steamed green beans, if liked.

---

1 **Pesto-Crusted Cod**
Heat 1 tablespoon olive oil in a flameproof skillet and cook 4 (5 oz) cod fillets for 2–3 minutes. Mix together ¼ cup fresh bread crumbs with ½ finely diced red chile, 2 tablespoons prepared pesto, and 3 sliced scallions. Spoon the bread crumb mixture over the fish and press down lightly. Sprinkle with 1 tablespoon grated Parmesan cheese and cook under a preheated hot broiler for 2–3 minutes, until golden and cooked through. Serve with a crisp green salad.

2 **Chili and Lemon Cod**
Slice 1 lemon and place a few slices on 4 pieces of parchment paper. Season 4 (5 oz) cod fillets with 1 teaspoon dried red pepper flakes, ¼ teaspoon smoked paprika, and a pinch of cayenne pepper. Place the cod fillets on top of the lemon slices. Make a package with the parchment paper, leaving one end open to pour 1 tablespoon white wine into each package. Seal the packages and place in an ovenproof dish. Cook in a preheated oven, at 400°F, for 15 minutes until cooked through. Remove the fish from the paper and serve with steamed green vegetables and any juices left in the packages.

Monkfish Wrapped in Prosciutto with Lentils and Spinach

Serves 4

4 skinless monkfish fillets, about 5 oz each
juice of 1 lemon
6–8 basil leaves, chopped, plus extra to garnish
2 teaspoons freshly ground black pepper
4 slices of prosciutto, halved lengthwise
¼ cup olive oil
2 shallots, diced
1 (15 oz) can green lentils, drained
1 (6 oz) package baby spinach
2 tablespoons crème fraîche or sour cream
salt

- Sprinkle the monkfish with half the lemon juice, basil, and pepper. Wrap each fillet in 2 slices of prosciutto and chill for 10 minutes.

- Meanwhile, heat half the olive oil in a skillet and sauté the shallots for 3–4 minutes. Stir in the lentils and cook for 2–3 minutes to heat through.

- Stir the spinach into the lentils, letting it wilt. Squeeze the remaining lemon juice over the lentils, stir in the crème fraîche, and season.

- Heat the remaining olive oil in another skillet and cook the wrapped monkfish for 6–8 minutes, turning over 2–3 times, until cooked through.

- Serve the wrapped monkfish on a bed of lentils and spinach, sprinkled with torn basil leaves.

---

10 Monkfish and Lentil Salad

Toss together 1 (5 oz) package baby spinach with 1 (15 oz) can green lentils, drained, 8 halved cherry tomatoes, and a few torn basil leaves in a salad bowl. Pan-fry 10 oz cubed monkfish in 1 tablespoon olive oil. Whisk together 3 tablespoons extra virgin olive oil, 1 tablespoon balsamic vinegar, a pinch of dried red pepper flakes, 1 teaspoon sugar, and 2 crushed garlic cloves. Add the monkfish to the salad, pour the dressing over the fish, then toss together. Serve sprinkled with 2 tablespoons toasted walnut pieces.

20 Monkfish Fillets in a Smoky Tomato

Sauce Heat 2 tablespoons olive oil in a skillet and sauté 2 finely diced shallots. Add 2 crushed garlic cloves, ½ teaspoon smoked paprika, and 1 cored, seeded, and thinly sliced red bell pepper. Pour in 1 (14½ oz) can diced tomatoes and simmer for 5–6 minutes. Stir in 3½ cups shredded spinach leaves and cook until wilted. Heat 1 tablespoon olive oil in another skillet and cook 1 lb monkfish fillet, cut into 1 inch chunks, for 1–2 minutes on each side. Transfer the monkfish to the tomato sauce and stir in gently.

Stir in 2 tablespoons chopped parsley and serve on a bed of cooked green lentils.

Tuna with Cannellini Bean and Roasted Red Pepper

Serves 4

3 red bell peppers, halved, cored, and seeded

1 (5 oz) can tuna in oil

½ teaspoon mustard

½ teaspoon honey

½ teaspoon balsamic vinegar

1 (15 oz) can cannellini beans, rinsed and drained

1 red onion, finely sliced

4 cherry tomatoes, halved

parsley leaves, to garnish

· Cook the red bell peppers, cut side down, under a preheated hot broiler, until the skins turn black. Place them in a large bowl, cover with plastic wrap, and let stand until cool enough to handle, then peel away the blackened skin. Slice the bell peppers.

· Drain the oil from the tuna into a bowl and whisk in the mustard, honey, and balsamic vinegar to taste.

· Using a fork, break up the tuna and divide among 4 plates. Add the strips of red bell pepper, drained cannellini beans, red onion, and cherry tomatoes.

· Pour the dressing over the salad and toss very briefly. Serve sprinkled with parsley leaves.

Bean, Red Pepper, and Shrimp Soup

Heat 1 tablespoon olive oil in a saucepan and sauté 1 chopped onion, 2 chopped garlic cloves, 2 cored, seeded, and chopped red bell peppers and 1 sliced carrot. Add 2 (15 oz) cans cannellini beans, rinsed and drained, and 4 cups hot vegetable stock. Bring to a boil, then simmer for 3–4 minutes. Using a handheld blender, or in a food processor or blender, blend the soup until smooth, then stir in 8 oz cooked, peeled shrimp and cook for 1 minute, until piping hot. Serve sprinkled with chopped basil leaves and a swirl of plain yogurt.

Seared Tuna with Broccoli, Bean, and Red Pepper Salad

Steam 3 cups broccoli florets until tender. Refresh under cold water. Whisk together 3 tablespoons extra virgin olive oil, 1 tablespoon balsamic vinegar, ½ teaspoon honey, ½ teaspoon mustard, and ½ teaspoon dried red pepper flakes in a bowl. Mix together 1 (15 oz) can lima beans, rinsed and drained, 1 cup sliced sun-dried tomatoes, 1 small diced red onion, and 1 cored, seeded, and diced red bell pepper in a salad bowl. Toss in the broccoli and dressing and mix well. Heat 2 tablespoons olive oil in a skillet and cook 4 (4 oz) tuna steaks for 2–3 minutes on each side. Let rest for 2 minutes before serving with the salad, sprinkled with 2 tablespoons toasted pine nuts and drizzled with 2 tablespoons olive oil.

ITA-FISH-QIW

30 Baked Trout with Olives

Serves 4

4 trout, about 8 oz each, scaled
¼ cup all-purpose flour
2 tablespoons olive oil
1 onion, sliced
⅓ cup pimento-stuffed green
  olives
3 tomatoes, diced
juice of 1 lemon
1 tablespoon capers
2 tablespoons chopped parsley,
  to garnish

- Dust the trout with flour. Heat the olive oil in a skillet and brown the trout for 2–3 minutes on each side. Place the fish in an ovenproof dish big enough for them to sit in a single layer.

- Add the onion and olives to the skillet, sauté for 3–4 minutes, and then spoon over the fish. Sprinkle the diced tomatoes, lemon juice, and capers over the fish and bake in a preheated oven, at 375 °F, for 15–18 minutes, until the fish is cooked through.

- Serve sprinkled with chopped parsley.

---

1 Smoked Trout Pâté

Place 12 oz flaked smoked trout, 1¾ sticks unsalted butter, the juice of 1 lemon, 1 tablespoon creamed horseradish, and a pinch of cayenne pepper into a food processor or blender and blend until smooth. Stir in another 4 oz flaked smoked trout with 1 tablespoon crème fraîche or sour cream and 2 tablespoons chopped chives. Serve with toasted ciabatta slices.

2 Creamy Smoked Trout and Pea Fusilli

Cook 16 oz fusilli in a saucepan of boiling water according to the package directions, until "al dente." Add 1¼ cups frozen peas for the last minute of cooking. Meanwhile, mix together 1 tablespoon creamed horseradish and ¼ cup crème fraîche or sour cream in a bowl. Flake 8 oz smoked trout fillets in another bowl. Drain the pasta and peas, return to the pan, and stir in the crème fraîche and trout. Season and serve with a green salad.

10 Sea Bass Fillets with Lentil Salad

Serves 4

¼ cup olive oil
1 (15 oz) can lentils, drained
2 tablespoons chopped parsley
1 red bell pepper, cored, seeded,
  and diced
3 scallions, sliced
1 pink grapefruit
4 sea bass fillets, about 5 oz each

- Heat 2 tablespoons of the olive oil in a small saucepan over medium heat. Add the lentils, parsley, red bell pepper, and scallions and cook for 2–3 minutes.

- Peel and segment the grapefruit over the pan to catch the juice, then mix the segments into the lentils.

- Heat the remaining olive oil in a skillet and cook the sea bass fillets for 2–3 minutes on each side, until cooked through.

- Serve on a bed of lentils.

---

20 Sea Bass Fillets with Crushed Olive

Potatoes Cook 1¼ lb chopped new potatoes in a saucepan of boiling water until tender. Meanwhile, heat 2 tablespoons olive oil in a skillet and cook 4 (5 oz) sea bass fillets, skin side down first, for 3–4 minutes on each side, until cooked through. Drain the potatoes, add 6 halved cherry tomatoes, 1 cup chopped, pitted ripe black olives, 3 tablespoons olive oil, and 1 tablespoon chopped parsley, and crush everything together with a fork. Divide the potatoes among 4 plates and top each one with a sea bass fillet.

30 Sea Bass Carpaccio

Slice a 1 lb skinless sea bass fillet very thinly, slightly on the diagonal, and place it in a shallow dish. Mix together the juice of 1 pink grapefruit, 3 tablespoons olive oil, 3 finely sliced scallions, and some pepper in a bowl, whisking to thicken. Pour the marinade over the slices of fish and let marinate for 25 minutes. Place the chopped leaves from 1 romaine heart on a serving dish and sprinkle with 2 peeled and segmented pink grapefuits. Spoon the marinated fish over the grapefruit segments and serve sprinkled with 1 tablespoon sesame seeds.

30 Saffron Scallops with Apple and Pistachio Puree

Serves 4

¼ cup olive oil
1 cinnamon stick
4 cloves
3 Pippin apples, peeled, cored, and chopped
1½ cups shelled pistachio nuts
juice of ½ lemon
1 tablespoon sherry vinegar
1 tablespoon honey
a small pinch of saffron threads
12 scallops

- Heat 1 tablespoon olive oil in a saucepan and cook the cinnamon stick and cloves for 1–2 minutes. Add the chopped apples. Cook over low heat for 4–5 minutes, until the apples are soft.

- Remove the spices and stir in half the pistachios and cook for another 3–4 minutes. Spoon the mixture into a food processor or blender and process until smooth. Stir in the lemon juice. Set aside and keep the puree warm.

- Put the remaining pistachios in a food processor or blender and process until finely chopped. Stir in 2 tablespoons olive oil.

- Heat the sherry vinegar in a small saucepan and simmer until reduced to 1 teaspoon. Stir in the honey and saffron.

- Heat the remaining olive oil in a skillet and sear the scallops for 1 minute on each side—do not overcook. Pour the saffron and honey glaze in the pan for the last 30 seconds.

- To serve, divide the apple and pistachio puree among 4 warm, shallow bowls. Top each one with 3 scallops, then drizzle the pistachio oil around them.

---

10 Scallop and Watercress Salad

Toss together 2 cups each of arugula, spinach, and watercress leaves, 1 thinly sliced apple, and 2 tablespoons Italian salad dressing. Heat 2 tablespoons sunflower oil in a skillet and sauté 6 sage leaves until crisp. Heat together a pat of butter and 1 tablespoon olive oil and cook 12 scallops for 1 minute on each side. Arrange the scallops over the greens, sprinkle with 1 tablespoon capers, 2 tablespoons chopped pistachio nuts, and the crispy sage leaves, and serve.

20 Bacon-Wrapped Scallops

Cut 6 bacon slices in half lengthwise, then wrap around 12 scallops. Use a toothpick to secure. Drizzle the scallops with lemon juice and place on a baking sheet. Bake in a preheated oven, at 375°F, for 15 minutes. Meanwhile, place 2 grated apples, 2 grated carrots, and ½ finely sliced green cabbage in a salad bowl and toss together with 2 tablespoons olive oil, 1 teaspoon honey, and the juice of ½ lemon. Sprinkle with 1 tablespoon chopped pistachio nuts. Serve the scallops with the coleslaw.

ITA-FISH-TIY

Creamy Mussels with Pancetta

Serves 4

4 slices of crusty Italian bread
3 garlic cloves, 1 whole, 2 crushed
2 tablespoons olive oil
8 oz pancetta or bacon, diced
3 lb mussels, cleaned
1 cup hard cider
3 tablespoons crème fraîche
  or sour cream
1 tablespoon chopped tarragon
1 tablespoon chopped parsley

- Toast the slices of bread on both sides, then rub each slice with the whole garlic clove and place in a warm, shallow bowl.

- Heat the olive oil in a large saucepan and cook the pancetta for 2–3 minutes, until crisp. Remove from the pan with a slotted spoon.

- Add the mussels to the pan with the crushed garlic and cider. Cover and let steam for 3–4 minutes, or until the mussels have opened. Discard any that do not open.

- Remove the mussels with a slotted spoon and place in the warm bowls over the toast.

- Add the crème fraîche to the mussel juices and boil for 1–2 minutes. Add the herbs and the prosciutto and warm through before pouring over the mussels and serving.

 Asparagus with Mussel Sauce

For the sauce, place 4 oz store-bought cooked, shelled mussels and 2 crushed garlic cloves in a small saucepan with ⅔ cup hot fish stock and simmer for 2 minutes. Add 1¼ cups heavy cream and 1 tablespoon chopped parsley and simmer for 4–5 minutes, until the sauce has thickened. Meanwhile, wrap 12 asparagus spears each in a slice of prosciutto and drizzle with 2 tablespoons olive oil. Heat a ridged grill pan and cook the asparagus for 4–5 minutes, turning occasionally, until chargrilled on all sides. Serve drizzled with the mussel sauce.

 Mussel and Saffron Risotto

Heat 2 tablespoons butter in a large saucepan and sauté 2 chopped shallots for 1 minute, then pour in ⅔ cup white wine. Bring to a simmer, add 2 lb cleaned mussels, cover, and cook for 2–3 minutes, until the mussels have opened. Discard any that do not open. Strain the mussels, reserving the cooking liquid in a large liquid measuring cup. Remove the mussels from their shells and set aside. Add fish stock to the reserved cooking liquid until you have 4 cups, add to a saucepan, and keep hot. Heat 2 tablespoons butter in a separate saucepan and sauté 2 chopped shallots for 2 minutes, then stir in 1½ cups risotto rice. Pour in a ladle of the reserved hot stock and add 2 pinches of saffron threads and cook, stirring continuously, until the liquid has all been absorbed. Repeat with the remaining hot stock, adding a ladle at a time, until the rice is "al dente." Stir in the reserved mussels and serve sprinkled with grated Parmesan cheese.

1 Shrimp and Tomato Salad

Serves 4

1 lb cooked, peeled jumbo shrimp

3 large tomatoes, diced

1 red bell pepper, cored, seeded, and chopped

4 scallions, sliced

1 cup arugula leaves

3 tablespoons extra virgin olive oil

2 tablespoons red wine vinegar

½ teaspoon cumin seeds

- Toss together the shrimp with the tomatoes, red bell pepper, scallions, and arugula leaves in a serving bowl.

- Whisk together the olive oil, red wine vinegar, and cumin seeds in a small bowl or jar.

- Pour the dressing over the salad and toss together to serve.

2 Shrimp with Beefsteak Tomato and Mozzarella

Slice 3 beefsteak tomatoes and 2 zucchini and cook on a hot ridged grill pan or barbecue until charred on each side. Layer the tomatoes and zucchini on a large platter with 8 oz sliced mozzarella cheese, 12 coarsely torn basil leaves, and 12 cooked, peeled jumbo shrimp. Drizzle 3 tablespoons extra virgin olive oil and the juice of ½ lemon over the salad and let stand for 5 minutes. Serve sprinkled with 2 tablespoons toasted pine nuts.

3 Shrimp-Stuffed Beefsteak

Tomatoes Heat 1 tablespoon olive oil in a skillet and sauté 2 chopped garlic cloves, 2 sliced scallions, and 10 cooked, peeled jumbo shrimp for 4–5 minutes. Mix in 2 cups fresh bread crumbs and 2 tablespoons chopped parsley and season to taste. Halve 4 beefsteak tomatoes horizontally and seed, then place in a roasting pan. Spoon the shrimp mixture into the tomatoes, then sprinkle with 2 tablespoons grated Parmesan cheese. Bake the stuffed tomatoes in a preheated oven, at 425°F, for 18–20 minutes. Serve with a green salad.

Pan-Fried Red Snapper with Green Beans

Serves 4

3 cups trimmed green beans

2 tablespoons olive oil

1 red onion, chopped

2 red bell peppers, cored, seeded, and sliced

4 red snapper fillets, about 5 oz each

2 tablespoons hazelnuts, chopped

2 tablespoons chopped parsley

- Steam or cook the green beans in a saucepan of boiling water until tender. Drain.

- Meanwhile, heat 1 tablespoon of the olive oil in a skillet and sauté the onion for 2–3 minutes, then add the red bell peppers and cook for another 2–3 minutes.

- Heat the remaining olive oil in another skillet and cook the red snapper fillets for 3–4 minutes on each side, until cooked through.

- Toss the steamed beans and the hazelnuts into the bell peppers, then remove from the heat and add the chopped parsley.

- Serve the fillets on a bed of green beans and bell peppers.

 Red Snapper with Tomato and Herb Sauce Heat 1 tablespoon olive oil in a skillet and cook 4 (5 oz) red snapper fillets for 3 minutes on each side, pouring in the juice of 1 orange when the fish is turned over. Remove the fish from the skillet and keep warm. Add 6 diced plum tomatoes, 1 tablespoon chopped tarragon, and 1 tablespoon chopped dill to the skillet and simmer for 3–4 minutes. Serve the fish with the tomato sauce.

Prosciutto-Wrapped Red Snapper with Crushed Potatoes Wrap 4 (5 oz) red snapper fillets each in 2 slices of overlapping prosciutto, with 2–3 basil leaves tucked inside each one. Cook 3 russet potatoes in a saucepan of boiling water until tender. Drain, add ½ cup chopped, pitted ripe black olives, 2 tablespoons olive oil, and some salt and pepper, and coarsely crush the potatoes with a fork. Meanwhile, toss 12 oz asparagus tips in 1 tablespoon olive oil, sauté for 4–5 minutes, until slightly charred, then remove and keep warm. Heat another 1 tablespoon olive oil in the skillet and cook the prosciutto-wrapped fish for 3–4 minutes on each side, until cooked through. Serve with the potatoes and asparagus.

ITA-FISH-LYC

Mixed Seafood Casserole

Serves 4

¼ cup olive oil
1 onion, diced
4 garlic cloves, crushed
½ cup white wine
1 (14½ oz) can diced tomatoes
1 cup fish stock
a pinch of saffron threads
1 lb prepared, cooked mixed
  seafood, thawed if frozen
2 tablespoons chopped parsley
crusty bread, to serve (optional)

- Heat the olive oil in a heavy saucepan and sauté the onion and garlic for 3–4 minutes. Pour in the white wine and boil for 2–3 minutes, then add the diced tomatoes, fish stock, and saffron.

- Bring to a simmer, stir in the mixed seafood and chopped parsley, and cook for 5–6 minutes to heat through.

- Serve with crusty bread, if liked.

Mixed Seafood Salad

Mix together 1 lb prepared, cooked mixed seafood, thawed if frozen, with 1 cored, seeded, and diced red bell pepper, 1 cored, seeded, and diced yellow bell pepper, 4 sliced scallions, 12 halved cherry tomatoes, and 2 cups arugula leaves in a salad bowl. Toss with 2 tablespoons olive oil and the juice of 1 lemon. Serve with crusty bread.

Seafood Risotto

Heat 2 tablespoons olive oil in a saucepan and sauté 1 diced onion, 1 finely diced red chile, and 2 crushed garlic cloves for 2–3 minutes. Stir in 2 cups risotto rice and 2 tablespoons tomato paste and cook for 1–2 minutes. Pour in ½ cup white wine and cook for 1–2 minutes, until it is absorbed. Add a ladle from a saucepan containing about 4 cups hot fish stock and stir continuously, until it has all been absorbed. Repeat with the remaining hot stock, adding a ladle at a time, until the rice is "al dente." Stir in 1 lb prepared, cooked mixed seafood, thawed if frozen, and a small handful of chopped parsley and cook for 2–3 minutes, or until the seafood is heated through. Squeeze in the juice of ½ lemon and serve immediately.

ITA-FISH-SEE

30 Marinated Sardines

Serves 4

12 butterflied sardines
½ cup olive oil
grated rind and juice of 1 lime
2 tablespoons chopped
  basil leaves
¼ teaspoon dried
  red pepper flakes

To serve

lemon wedges
ciabatta bread or crunchy green
  salad (optional)

- Place the sardines in a shallow nonmetallic dish.

- Whisk together the olive oil, lime juice, basil, and dried red pepper flakes in a small bowl or jar and pour the marinade over the sardines. Cover with plastic wrap and chill for 20 minutes.

- Cook the sardine fillets under a preheated hot broiler for 1–2 minutes on each side, until cooked through.

- Serve with lemon wedges and ciabatta bread or crunchy green salad, if desired.

 Sardine and Tomato Bruschetta

Lightly toast 8 slices of ciabatta on both sides, then rub each slice with a garlic clove. Slice 3 tomatoes thinly and lay the slices on the toast. Place a few arugula leaves on each. Top the bruschetta with 2 (3¾ oz) cans sardines in oil, drained and oil reserved. Drizzle with the oil from the cans and season with pepper.

 Sardines with Lima Beans

Dip 8 sardines in seasoned flour. Heat 2 tablespoons olive oil in a large skillet and cook the floured sardines for 3 minutes on each side, until cooked through. Remove from the skillet and keep warm. Add 1 tablespoon olive oil to the skillet and sauté 2 finely chopped garlic cloves for 1 minute, then add ½ cup white wine and boil for 1 minute, scraping any sediment off the bottom of the skillet. Add 1 (15 oz) can lima beans, rinsed and drained, 12 cherry tomatoes, and 3 tablespoons chopped parsley. Return the sardines to the skillet, squeeze the juice of 1 lemon over them, and season. Serve with crusty bread to mop up the juices.

Tuna and Cannellini Bean Salad

Serves 4

1 (12 oz) can tuna, drained
1 tomato, diced
¼ cup pitted ripe black olives
1 (15 oz) can cannellini beans, rinsed and drained
1 red onion, sliced
2 cups arugula leaves
extra virgin olive oil, to serve

- Place the tuna in a serving bowl and break it into chunks using a fork.

- Mix in the diced tomatoes, black olives, cannellini beans, red onion, and arugula leaves.

- Drizzle with olive oil and serve immediately.

 Speedy Tuna and Green Bean Salad

Make the Green Bean Salad (see right). Gently stir in 1 (12 oz) can drained and flaked tuna chunks.

 Pan-Fried Tuna with Green Bean Salad Place 4 (5 oz) tuna steaks on a board and season both sides with pepper. Steam 1 lb green beans for 4–5 minutes. Meanwhile, whisk together 3 tablespoons extra virgin olive oil with the juice of 1 lemon and ½ teaspoon honey in a salad bowl. Stir in 1 cup chopped sun-dried tomatoes and ½ cup pitted and sliced ripe black olives. Toss the warm steamed beans in the dressing. Toast ½ cup hazelnuts in a dry skillet until golden, then coarsely chop them and toss into the beans. Heat 1 tablespoon olive oil in a skillet and cook the tuna for 3–4 minutes on each side, depending on how rare you like your tuna. Serve the pan-fried tuna on a bed of the bean salad.

ITA-FISH-XOS

QuickCook
Meat and Poultry

Recipes listed by cooking time

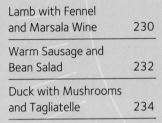

30 Lamb and Olive Stew

Serves 4

1 lb shoulder of lamb,
 cut into small cubes

2 tablespoons flour, seasoned

2 tablespoons olive oil

1 onion, chopped

2 carrots, diced

2 garlic cloves, chopped

½ tablespoon chopped rosemary

1 cup white wine

1 (14½ oz) can diced tomatoes

12 ripe black olives, pitted

grated rind and juice of 1 lemon

2 tablespoons chopped parsley

3½ cups water

1¼ cups instant polenta

2 tablespoons butter

2 tablespoons grated Parmesan
 cheese

- Dust the cubes of lamb with the seasoned flour. Heat the olive oil in a saucepan and brown the meat all over.

- Add the onions and cook for 3–4 minutes, stirring, then add the carrots, garlic, and rosemary. Cook for 3–4 minutes.

- Pour in the white wine and diced tomatoes, bring to a boil, and then simmer for 20 minutes, until the lamb is tender.

- Stir in the olives, lemon rind and juice, and chopped parsley 1 minute before the end of cooking.

- Meanwhile, bring the measured water to boil in another saucepan and pour in the polenta. Cook, stirring continuously, for 1 minute. Stir in the butter and grated Parmesan and divide among 4 bowls.

- Spoon the lamb stew over the polenta and serve.

 Lamb Cutlets with Fried Polenta
Heat 2 tablespoons olive oil in a skillet and sauté 8 slices of block polenta for 2 minutes on each side. Remove and keep warm. Add 1 tablespoon olive oil to the same skillet and sauté 1 finely diced onion and 1 finely diced red chile for 1 minute before adding 8 lamb cutlets and a sprinkling of dried oregano. Cook the lamb for 2 minutes on each side. Sprinkle in a dash of red wine and 2 tablespoons chopped ripe black olives. Serve the cutlets with the fried polenta.

 Rack of Lamb with Rosemary and Olives Heat 1 tablespoon olive oil in a skillet and brown 2 (1½ lb–2 lb) racks of lamb. Place them both in a roasting pan and pour 1¼ cups white wine over the lamb and sprinkle with 2–3 rosemary sprigs, 30 pitted ripe black olives, and 3 tablespoons capers. Cook in a preheated oven, at 400°F, for 15 minutes. Meanwhile, steam 3 cups broccoli florets and 2 sliced zucchini. Serve the lamb carved into cutlets with the juices from the pan and a side dish of steamed green vegetables.

30 Beef Carpaccio

Serves 4

1 beef tenderloin steak,
about 8 oz

3 tablespoons extra virgin
olive oil

1 teaspoon freshly ground
black pepper

1 tablespoon chopped thyme
leaves

1 teaspoon Dijon mustard

½ tablespoon balsamic vinegar

½ teaspoon honey

2 cups arugula leaves

¼ cup Parmesan cheese shavings,
to serve

- Place the steak on a cutting board and rub with 1 tablespoon of the olive oil, the pepper, and thyme. Wrap in plastic wrap and place in the freezer for 20 minutes.

- Meanwhile, whisk together the remaining olive oil, mustard, balsamic vinegar, and honey in a bowl. Arrange the arugula on a serving plate.

- Unwrap the steak, slice it as thinly as possible, and then arrange over the arugula leaves.

- Serve sprinkled with Parmesan shavings and drizzled with the dressing.

Steak Sandwich
Rub 1 lb top sirloin steak with olive oil and season with pepper. Heat a ridged grill pan until very hot and cook the steak for 3–4 minutes on each side. Let rest. Meanwhile, cook 1 sliced red onion in the grill pan for 1–2 minutes, then toast the cut sides of 4 halved ciabatta rolls in the pan. Spread the roll bottoms with 1 tablespoon mayonnaise mixed with 1 teaspoon whole-grain mustard and then top with a small bunch of arugula and the cooked onion. Slice the steak and place on top. Top with the other half of the ciabatta rolls and serve.

Grilled Beef Salad
Whisk together 3 tablespoons extra virgin olive oil, 1 tablespoon balsamic vinegar, ½ teaspoon creamed horseradish, and ½ teaspoon honey in a small bowl. Heat a ridged grill pan or barbecue and cook 1 lb top sirloin steak until cooked to your liking. Let rest. Toss together 3 cups mixed salad greens, 2 thinly sliced and halved beefsteak tomatoes, 2 sliced avocados, and 1 cored, seeded, and sliced yellow bell pepper in a bowl. Divide the salad among 4 plates. Slice the steak and arrange on top of the salad. Drizzle with the horseradish dressing to serve.

30 Chicken Parmesan

Serves 4

4 boneless, skinless chicken
  breasts, about 5 oz each
2 tablespoons all-purpose flour
2 eggs, beaten
2 cups fresh bread crumbs
¾ cup grated Parmesan cheese
3 tablespoons olive oil
1 onion, diced
2 garlic cloves, crushed
1 (14½ oz) can diced tomatoes
1 teaspoon dried oregano
¼ teaspoon dried red
  pepper flakes
8–10 basil leaves, shredded
8 oz mozzarella cheese, sliced

- Place each chicken breast between 2 pieces of plastic wrap and, using a meat mallet or rolling pin, flatten each one to an even thickness of about ½ inch.

- Place the flour in one shallow bowl, the eggs in another, and the bread crumbs and Parmesan mixed together in a third.

- Dip each chicken breast first in the flour, then the egg, and finally the bread crumb and Parmesan mixture so that it is completely coated. Chill for a few minutes.

- Heat 1 tablespoon of the olive oil in a skillet and sauté the onion and garlic for 2–3 minutes. Add the diced tomatoes, oregano, and red pepper flakes and simmer for 10 minutes.

- Meanwhile, heat the remaining olive oil in another skillet and cook the chicken breasts for 4–5 minutes on each side, until golden.

- Pour the tomato sauce into an ovenproof dish. Place the chicken on top and sprinkle with the basil. Top each one with slices of mozzarella and bake in a preheated oven, at 400°F, for 10 minutes, or until the mozzarella is melted and golden and the chicken cooked through.

 Quick Chicken Salad Coarsely shred 3 store-bought, cooked chicken breasts. Mix in a bowl with 2 sliced mangoes, 2 cups arugula, and 1 cup coarsely chopped Fontina or other hard cheese. Whisk together 3 tablespoons olive oil, 1 tablespoon balsamic vinegar, and ½ teaspoon mustard. Pour the dressing over the salad and sprinkle with 2 tablespoons toasted pumpkin seeds to serve.

 Chicken and Parmesan Soup Heat 1 tablespoon olive oil in a saucepan and add 1 diced onion, 2 crushed garlic cloves, and 2 diced boneless, skinless chicken breasts. Cook for 5–6 minutes, stirring occasionally. Pour in 3 cups chicken stock, ½ cup white wine, and 1 (14½ oz) can diced tomatoes. Bring to a simmer and cook for 12 minutes. Stir in 3 tablespoons grated Parmesan cheese and 2 tablespoons shredded basil leaves. Serve with crusty bread.

Veal with Prosciutto and Sage

Serves 4

4 veal cutlets, about 5 oz each
4 slices of prosciutto
4 sage leaves
2 tablespoons flour
3 tablespoons olive oil
3 cups trimmed green beans
grated rind of 1 lemon
2 tablespoons butter
½ cup white wine
salt and pepper

- Place each veal cutlet between 2 pieces of plastic wrap and, using a meat mallet or rolling pin, flatten each one to an even thickness of about ¼ inch.

- Place a slice of prosciutto and a sage leaf on top of each scallop and hold in place with a toothpick.

- Place the flour on a plate and season well. Toss each scallop in the seasoned flour.

- Steam the green beans and toss in 1 tablespoon of the olive oil and the lemon rind and keep warm.

- Heat the butter and the remaining olive oil in a skillet and cook the scallops for 2–3 minutes on each side.

- Remove the scallops from the skillet and pour in the wine, scraping all the sediment from the bottom of the skillet. Boil for 1–2 minutes.

- Serve the scallops on a bed of green beans with the sauce poured over them.

1 Green Bean and Prosciutto Salad

Steam 1 lb green beans and cook 8 slices of prosciutto in 1 tablespoon olive oil until crisp. Gently toss together the steamed green beans, 2 chopped avocados, 6 halved cherry tomatoes, 2 tablespoons toasted pine nuts, and 8 oz mozzarella cheese, torn. Drizzle with 3 tablespoons olive oil and the juice of ½ lemon, then top with the coarsely chopped prosciutto.

3 Creamy Veal with Tagliatelle and Crisp Prosciutto

Cook 16 oz tagliatelle in a saucepan of boiling water according to the package directions, until "al dente." Meanwhile, cut 1 lb veal cutlets into strips and coat with seasoned flour. Heat 2 tablespoons olive oil in a skillet and cook the veal for 6–7 minutes, until browned. Remove from the skillet and keep warm. Add 1 chopped onion to the skillet and sauté for about 10 minutes, until golden. Pour in ½ cup white wine and simmer for 4–5 minutes before adding 1 cup light cream, 2–3 tablespoons chicken stock, and 2 skinned, seeded, and diced tomatoes. Meanwhile, cook 8 slices of prosciutto under a preheated hot broiler for 3–4 minutes on each side, until crisp. Return the veal to the skillet with the drained pasta and 2 tablespoons chopped parsley. Toss together and serve topped with the crisp prosciutto and sprinkled with 2 tablespoons grated Parmesan cheese.

30 Lemon and Rosemary Pork with Cannellini Bean Salad

Serves 4

1 tablespoon olive oil

2 teaspoons finely chopped rosemary

4 garlic cloves, crushed

grated rind and juice of 1 lemon

4 boneless pork chops, about 5 oz each

1 red onion, sliced

2 tablespoons sherry vinegar

2 (15 oz) cans cannellini beans, drained and rinsed

4 cups mixed salad greens

- Mix together the olive oil, rosemary, garlic, and lemon juice in a nonmetallic bowl. Add the pork chops and toss in the oil to coat. Let stand for 10 minutes.

- Heat a ridged grill pan and cook the pork chops for 3–4 minutes on each side, until cooked through. Remove from the pan and keep warm.

- Pour the remainder of the marinade into the pan, add the onion, and cook for 2–3 minutes, then pour in the sherry vinegar and boil for 1–2 minutes.

- Stir in the drained cannellini beans and heat through.

- Toss the beans with the salad greens and serve with the pork.

 Pancetta and Cannellini Bean Salad Heat 2 tablespoons olive oil in a skillet and sauté 1 sliced red onion, 4 oz diced pancetta, and 2 crushed garlic cloves for 2–3 minutes. Add 1 cored, seeded, and diced red bell pepper and cook for another 1 minute. Pour in 2 (15 oz) cans cannellini beans, drained and rinsed, and cook for 1–2 minutes to heat through. Stir in 2 tablespoons shredded basil leaves, some salt and pepper, and the juice of ½ lemon to serve.

 Parmesan Pork Chops with Cannellini Beans Lay 4 (6 oz) pork chops between 2 pieces of plastic wrap and, using a meat mallet or rolling pin, flatten each one to an even thickness of about ½ inch. Mix together ½ cup fresh bread crumbs, a small handful of chopped sage, and 2 tablespoons grated Parmesan cheese in a shallow dish. Put 1 beaten egg in another shallow dish. Dip each pork chop first into the egg and then into the bread crumb mixture to coat. Heat 2 tablespoons olive oil in a skillet and cook the pork chops for 3–4 minutes on each side, until golden. Meanwhile, heat 1 (15 oz) can cannellini beans, rinsed and drained, in a small saucepan, then stir in 1 tablespoon olive oil and 1 tablespoon chopped parsley. Serve the pork chops with the beans and steamed cabbage.

Lamb-Stuffed Pita Pockets

Serves 4

1 cup arugula leaves

20 green olives, pitted and sliced

2 red bell peppers, cored, seeded, and sliced

2 avocados, pitted and chopped

2 tomatoes, chopped

4 scallions, sliced

1 tablespoon Italian salad dressing

4 pita breads

2 cups bite-size, leftover cooked lamb pieces

- Mix together the arugula leaves, olives, red bell peppers, avocados, tomatoes, and scallions in a bowl.

- Toss in the Italian salad dressing.

- Cook the pita breads under a preheated hot broiler for 1–2 minutes. While they are still warm, run a knife down one side and slice them open to make 4 pockets.

- Divide the cooked lamb among each pita and then spoon in the salad to serve.

 Meat-Topped Pizzas

Heat 1 tablespoon olive oil in a skillet and sauté 1 diced onion, 1 cored, seeded, and sliced red bell pepper, and 2 crushed garlic cloves for 1–2 minutes. Stir in 1 lb ground beef and brown the meat. Add 1 (14½ oz) can diced tomatoes and 2 tablespoons tomato paste and simmer for 3–4 minutes. Spoon the mixture over 4 store-bought individual pizza crusts, sprinkle with 3 cups shredded mozzarella cheese, and bake in a preheated oven, at 425°F, for 11–12 minutes, until golden.

 Meat-Filled Calzones

To make the dough, place 3⅔ cups white bread flour, 2¼ teaspoons active dry yeast, and a pinch of salt in a large bowl and mix together. Make a well in the center. Stir in 1 tablespoon olive oil and most of 1¼ cups warm water. Mix together with your hand, adding more water, if necessary, until you have a soft but not sticky dough. Turn out the dough onto a floured work surface and knead for 5–10 minutes, until the dough is smooth and elastic. Divide into 4 pieces and roll out to 8 inch circles. Mix together

8 halved cherry tomatoes, 2 cups chopped mozzarella cheese, 4 oz prosciutto, 4 oz salami, 1 tablespoon capers, and ½ cup grated Parmesan cheese in a bowl. Divide among the 4 circles of dough, placing the mixture onto one half of each circle and leaving a 1 inch clean edge. Brush the clean edges of the dough with water and then fold the other half over the filling and pinch together the edges to seal. Place the calzones on a large baking sheet and bake in a preheated oven, at 425°F, for 6–8 minutes, until the dough is cooked and the filling is hot.

 # Sage Liver and Mashed Potatoes

Serves 4

1 (28 oz) package store-bought or 4 cups homemade mashed potatoes

1 lb lamb's liver, sliced thinly

2 tablespoons flour, seasoned

4 tablespoons butter

4–5 sage leaves, chopped·

- Heat the mashed potatoes according to the package directions.

- Meanwhile, dust the liver in the seasoned flour.

- Heat the butter in a skillet and cook the liver with the sage leaves for 1–2 minutes on each side.

- Serve with the warm mashed potatoes, pouring the butter and juices over the potatoes.

 ### Liver with Mushrooms

Dust 1 lb thinly sliced calf's liver with 2 tablespoons all-purpose flour seasoned with salt and pepper. Heat 1 tablespoon olive oil in a skillet and cook the liver for 2 minutes on each side. Remove and keep warm. Heat another 1 tablespoon olive oil in a clean skillet and sauté 1 sliced onion and 2 cups sliced cremini mushrooms for 4–5 minutes. Meanwhile, bring 3½ cups water to a boil in a saucepan. Pour in 1¼ cups instant polenta and cook for 1–2 minutes, stirring continuously, until it thickens. Prepare 1 tablespoon chopped chives and 1 tablespoon chopped parsley and stir half of these into the polenta. Add the remaining herbs to the mushroom mixture and then add the liver and the juice of 1 lemon and heat for 1 minute. Serve the liver and mushrooms spooned over the herb polenta.

 ### Liver with Tomatoes and

Pasta Heat 1 tablespoon olive oil in a skillet and sauté 1 sliced onion with 4 chopped bacon slices for 3–4 minutes. Add 1 (14½ oz) can diced tomatoes, 1 tablespoon Worcestershire sauce, 1 tablespoon tomato paste, ¼ teaspoon dried mixed herbs, and ⅔ cup vegetable stock. Bring to a boil and simmer for 12–15 minutes. Meanwhile, heat 4 tablespoons butter in another skillet and cook 1 lb thinly sliced and floured calf's liver for 1–2 minutes on each side. Cook 12 oz tagliatelle in a saucepan of boiling water according to the package directions, until "al dente." Drain and divide among 4 plates. Add the liver to the tomato sauce and serve poured over the pasta.

ITA-MEAT-WYM

10 Quick Chicken Liver Salad

Serves 4

4 bacon slices
1 lb chicken livers, trimmed
1 tablespoon extra virgin olive oil
1 cup watercress or arugula
1 romaine lettuce, leaves torn
1 red onion, thinly sliced
salt and pepper
Italian salad dressing, to serve

- Cook the bacon slices under a preheated hot broiler until crisp. Let cool, then chop coarsely.

- Meanwhile, season the chicken livers.

- Heat the olive oil in a skillet and cook the chicken livers until golden but still pink in the middle. Let cool slightly, then cut into bite-size pieces.

- Toss together the watercress, torn lettuce leaves, and red onion in a large bowl.

- Add the chicken livers and chopped bacon, drizzle with Italian salad dressing, and serve immediately.

---

 2 Calf's Liver with Caramelized Onions Heat 2 tablespoons olive oil and 2 tablespoons butter in a skillet and stir in 3 sliced large onions. Cook over medium heat for 15 minutes, stirring frequently. Add a dash of balsamic vinegar and 1 tablespoon dark brown sugar and cook for another 3–4 minutes. Meanwhile, heat 2 tablespoons olive oil and 2½ tablespoons butter in another skillet and cook 1 lb calf's liver for 2–3 minutes on each side. Serve with the onions spooned over.

 3 Calf's Liver with Sage and Mashed Potatoes Peel 7 russet or Yukon gald potatoes (1¾ lb) and cut them into equal chunks. Cook the potatoes in a saucepan of boiling water until tender. Heat 2 tablespoons olive oil and 2½ tablespoons butter in a skillet and sauté 8–10 sage leaves until crispy. Remove from the skillet and drain on paper towels. Drain the potatoes, mash them with 2 tablespoons crème fraîche or cream, and keep warm. Cook 1 lb calf's liver in the same skillet used for the sage for 2–3 minutes on each side. Meanwhile, heat another 2 tablespoons olive oil in a clean skillet and cook 1 lb baby spinach leaves until they start to wilt. Divide the mashed potatoes among 4 plates, top with the wilted spinach, then the liver, and finally the sage leaves. Pour any juices from the pan over the liver and serve immediately.

Polenta-Crusted Pork with Pear and Arugula Salad

Serves 4

¼ cup instant polenta
¼ cup grated Parmesan cheese
2 tablespoons all-purpose flour
1 egg, beaten
4 pork cutlets, about 5 oz each
3 pears, cored and sliced
1 red onion, sliced
3 cups arugula leaves
2 tablespoons walnut pieces
3 tablespoons olive oil
1 tablespoon balsamic vinegar
4 tablespoons butter

- Mix together the polenta and Parmesan and place in a shallow bowl. Place the flour and egg in separate bowls.

- Dip the pork cutlets into the flour, then the egg, and finally coat with the polenta. Chill for 5 minutes.

- Place the pears, onion, arugula, and walnuts in a bowl and toss with 2 tablespoons of the olive oil and the balsamic vinegar.

- Heat the remaining olive oil and butter in a skillet and cook the pork cutlets for 3–4 minutes on each side, until golden and cooked through.

- Serve on a bed of the dressed salad.

Pork Chops with Pan-Fried Polenta and Deviled Tomatoes

Sprinkle 4 halved, large tomatoes with ½ teaspoon garam masala, 1 crushed garlic clove, and some salt and pepper. Drizzle with 1 tablespoon olive oil and cook under a preheated hot broiler for 4–5 minutes, until cooked. Meanwhile, heat 2 tablespoons olive oil in a large skillet and cook 12 oz prepared block polenta, cut into thick slices, and 4 (5 oz) pork loin chops for 3–4 minutes on each side, until golden and cooked through. Sprinkle with 1 tablespoon chopped basil leaves for the last minute of cooking. Serve the pork chops with the polenta, topped with the spiced tomatoes.

Pork Chops with Pears

Heat 2 tablespoons olive oil in a roasting pan on the stove and cook 2 red onions cut into wedges, 2 cored and quartered pears, and a few sprigs of rosemary. Add 4 (5 oz) pork chops and cook for 2–3 minutes on each side, until cooked through. Crumble ⅓ cup Gorgonzola cheese over the pork and place the pan under a preheated hot broiler and cook until the cheese starts to melt. Serve with green vegetables.

30 Honey, Mustard, and Lemon Lamb

Serves 4

4 garlic cloves, crushed

¼ cup honey

2 tablespoons whole-grain mustard

grated rind and juice of 1 lemon

a small handful of rosemary, chopped

2 tablespoons olive oil

4 lamb cutlets, about 5 oz each

12 oz tagliatelle

1 red onion, sliced

2 zucchini, sliced

- Whisk together the garlic, honey, mustard, lemon rind and juice, rosemary, and 1 tablespoon of the olive oil in a nonmetallic bowl. Toss the lamb in the marinade and let stand for 10 minutes.

- Cook the tagliatelle in a saucepan of boiling water according to the package directions, until "al dente."

- Meanwhile, cook the lamb under a preheated hot broiler for 3–4 minutes on each side, or until cooked to your liking.

- Heat the remaining olive oil in a skillet and sauté the onion and zucchini for 3–4 minutes, then pour in the remaining marinade. Simmer for 1–2 minutes.

- Drain the pasta and toss into the skillet with the sliced onion and zucchini.

- Serve the lamb cutlets with the tagliatelle.

 1 Lamb and Asparagus Salad

Whisk together 3 tablespoons extra virgin olive oil, 1 tablespoon lemon juice, ½ teaspoon whole-grain mustard, and ½ teaspoon honey in a bowl. Toss 12 oz asparagus tips in ½ tablespoon olive oil and cook in a hot ridged grill pan for 1–2 minutes. Place the asparagus on a bed of watercress, arugula, and spinach leaves and top with 2 cups bite-size, cooked lamb slices. Sprinkle with 1⅓ cups crumbled feta cheese and drizzle with the dressing to serve.

 2 Italian Lamb Kebabs

Mix together 8 oz ground lamb, ½ teaspoon fennel seeds, 1 crushed garlic clove, ½ tablespoon chopped basil leaves, and salt and pepper in a large bowl. Divide the mixture into 8 balls, then thread 2 each onto 4 metal skewers and brush with oil. Cook on a preheated, hot ridged grill pan for 8–10 minutes, turning until cooked all over. Serve with a crisp salad and a dressing made with 3 tablespoons extra virgin olive oil, the juice of ½ lemon, ½ teaspoon Dijon mustard, and ½ teaspoon honey.

Roman Chicken with Bell Peppers

Serves 4

3 tablespoons olive oil

4 boneless, skinless chicken breasts, about 5 oz each

1 red onion, sliced

3 garlic cloves, crushed

2 red bell peppers, cored, seeded, and sliced

1 yellow bell pepper, cored, seeded, and sliced

1 green bell pepper, cored, seeded, and sliced

1¼ cups pitted green olives

3 cups cherry tomatoes

1¼ cups chicken stock

2 oregano sprigs

2 tablespoons chopped parsley

salt and pepper

- Heat the olive oil in a flameproof casserole and brown the chicken. Remove and set aside.

- Add the onion and garlic and sauté for 1–2 minutes. Add the bell peppers and cook for another 2–3 minutes, then add the olives, cherry tomatoes, stock, and oregano.

- Return the chicken to the casserole, bring to a simmer, and cook for 20–22 minutes, covered, until the chicken is cooked through and tender.

- Stir in the chopped parsley, then season and serve.

 Chicken and Bell Pepper Salad

Toss together 2 cored, seeded, and sliced red bell peppers with 3 diced tomatoes, 2 sliced avocados, and a handful of baby spinach in a salad bowl. Top with 3 store-bought, cooked and sliced chicken breasts and 4 slices of pancetta that have been broiled until crisp. Drizzle with Italian salad dressing and serve with crusty bread.

 Chicken and Red Pepper Panini

Halve, core, and seed 3 red bell peppers and cook, cut side down, under a preheated hot broiler, until the skin turns black. Place in a bowl and cover with plastic wrap until cool enough to peel away the blackened skin. Cut into strips. Meanwhile, mix together ¼ cup mayonnaise with 1 tablespoon pesto. Cut 2 ciabatta loaves in half horizontally and spread each cut side with the pesto mayonnaise. Place a small handful of baby spinach leaves and 8 oz sliced mozzarella cheese on the bottom half of each loaf. Top with 3 store-bought, cooked and sliced chicken breasts, 4 sliced tomatoes, the red bell pepper strips, and a few basil leaves. Top with the other half of the loaf. Place both loaves on a hot ridged grill pan, pressing down with a spatula to flatten. Cook for about 3 minutes on each side, until the cheese starts to melt. Cut in half and serve hot.

Broiled Lamb with Anchovy Sauce

Serves 4

10–12 anchovy fillets
juice of 1 lemon
2 teaspoons chopped rosemary
¼ cup olive oil
8 lamb chops, about 5 oz each
1 lb baby broccoli
pepper

- Place the anchovies in a mortar and pestle and pound them to a paste. Gradually add the lemon juice, followed by the rosemary and olive oil, until you have a creamy dressing. This can also be made in a food processor or blender.

- Season the lamb chops with pepper and cook under a preheated hot broiler for 3–4 minutes on each side, or until cooked to your liking.

- Steam the broccoli for 3–4 minutes, until tender.

- Drizzle the lamb chops with the anchovy sauce and serve with the steamed broccoli.

Spaghetti with Lamb, Broccoli, and Anchovies

Cook 12 oz spaghetti in a saucepan of boiling water according to the package directions, until "al dente." Add ½ bunch of broccoli, cut into florets, for the last 3 minutes of cooking. Meanwhile, heat 3 tablespoons olive oil in a skillet and cook 8 chopped anchovies and 1 finely chopped red chile with 4 (5 oz) sliced lamb loin chops for about 3–4 minutes. Add 2 cups bread crumbs and cook, stirring, until the bread crumbs are golden. Drain the spaghetti and broccoli and return to the skillet with half the bread crumb mixture and toss well with 2 tablespoons olive oil. Serve sprinkled with the remaining crumbs.

Lamb Caesar Salad with Anchovies

For the dressing, blend together 1 finely chopped garlic clove, 1 teaspoon Dijon mustard, ½ teaspoon Worcestershire sauce, 1 tablespoon lemon juice, 4 anchovy fillets, 3 tablespoons mayonnaise, and ¼ cup plain yogurt. Toss 4 (5 oz) sliced lamb cutlets in 1 tablespoon olive oil, 2 teaspoons chopped thyme leaves, the juice of ½ lemon, 1 crushed garlic clove, and some pepper. Cook in a preheated hot ridged grill pan for 5–6 minutes. Heat 2 tablespoons olive oil in a skillet and cook 3 cups of bread cubes cut from a ciabatta loaf, until golden. Roughly tear the leaves of 2 romaine lettuce and place in a large bowl or platter. Add the cooked lamb, 6 anchovy fillets, and the croutons. Spoon the dressing over the salad and gently toss together before serving topped with 3 tablespoons Parmesan cheese shavings.

Meatballs with Tomato Sauce and Spaghetti

Serves 4

1 lb ground sirloin beef
5 garlic cloves, crushed
¼ teaspoon dried oregano
1 tablespoon chopped parsley
2 tablespoons grated
   Parmesan cheese
2 tablespoons olive oil
1 onion, diced
a small pinch of dried red
   pepper flakes
2 (14½ oz) can diced tomatoes
½ cup red wine
1 teaspoon sugar
2 tablespoons chopped
   basil leaves
16 oz spaghetti
Parmesan cheese shavings,
   to serve

- Mix together the ground beef, 2 of the crushed garlic cloves, the oregano, chopped parsley, and grated Parmesan in a mixing bowl. Roll into walnut-size balls.

- Heat 1 tablespoon of the olive oil in a skillet and sauté the meatballs for 10–12 minutes, turning frequently.

- In another skillet, heat the remaining olive oil and sauté the onion, remaining crushed garlic, and red pepper flakes for 3–4 minutes, then add the diced tomatoes, red wine, sugar, and basil and simmer for 8–10 minutes.

- Meanwhile, cook the spaghetti in a saucepan of boiling water according to the package directions, until "al dente."

- Transfer the meatballs to the tomato sauce and cook for another 3–4 minutes, until cooked through.

- Drain the spaghetti and serve the meatballs spooned over the top. Serve sprinkled with Parmesan shavings.

Quick Spaghetti Bolognese Cook 16 oz thin spaghetti according to package directions, until "al dente." Meanwhile, heat 1 tablespoon olive oil in a skillet and sauté 1 diced red onion and 1 diced red chile for 30 seconds. Stir in 10 oz ground sirloin beef and cook over high heat for 2–3 minutes. Stir in 1¾ cups prepared tomato-based pasta sauce and simmer for 3–4 minutes. Drain the pasta and divide among 4 bowls. Top with the sauce, 2 tablespoons shredded basil leaves, and 2 tablespoons grated Parmesan.

Chicken Meatballs Heat 1 tablespoon olive oil in a skillet and cook 1 lb ground chicken with ⅓ cup pine nuts for 5–6 minutes. Remove from the heat and place in a bowl with 1 tablespoon chopped basil leaves, 2 cups fresh bread crumbs, ½ cup grated Parmesan cheese, 2 beaten eggs, and the grated rind and juice of 1 lemon. Use your hands to bring together the mixture, then divide into walnut-size balls. Heat another 1 tablespoon olive oil in a skillet and cook the meatballs until brown all over and cooked through. Serve with 2 cups warmed, store-bought tomato-based pasta sauce, sprinkled with chopped parsley.

30 Creamy Veal Cutlets

Serves 4

1/3 oz dried porcini
4 veal cutlets, about 5 oz each
2 tablespoons all-purpose flour
4 tablespoons butter
1 tablespoon olive oil
2 garlic cloves, chopped
1 onion, chopped
1½ cups sliced cremini
  mushrooms
½ cup white wine
1 cup light cream
a large handful of baby spinach
  leaves
salt and pepper
mashed potatoes, to serve

- Soak the porcini in just enough boiling water to cover for 10 minutes. Drain, reserving the liquid, and coarsely chop.

- Pound the cutlets with a meat mallet or rolling pin until thin. Dust the veal scallops with the flour. Heat the butter and the olive oil in a skillet and cook the scallops for 2–3 minutes on each side, until just cooked through. Remove from the skillet and keep warm.

- Add the garlic, onion, and mushrooms to the skillet and sauté for 4–5 minutes, until the onion is soft.

- Pour in the wine and simmer for 2–3 minutes, then pour in the cream and 2–3 tablespoons of the reserved porcini liquid.

- Bring to a boil, then stir in the porcini and spinach and some salt and pepper. Return the scallops to the skillet and cook for 1 minute before serving with mashed potatoes.

 Veal Salad

Heat 1 tablespoon olive oil in a skillet and cook a 10 oz veal cutlet for 2–3 minutes on each side, or until cooked to your liking. Rest for 1–2 minutes, then slice thinly against the grain. In a large salad bowl, toss the veal with 2 chopped beefsteak tomatoes, 2 cups mixed lettuce, ¾ cup arugula, 2 tablespoons chopped walnuts, and ½ cup sliced roasted peppers from a jar. Serve dressed with 2–3 tablespoons Italian salad dressing and sprinkled with 3 tablespoons Parmesan cheese shavings.

 Veal Porcini with Pasta

Cook 12 oz pappardelle pasta in a saucepan of boiling water according to the package directions, until "al dente." Meanwhile, heat 2 tablespoons olive oil in a large skillet and sauté 2 diced shallots and 1 crushed garlic clove. Add 8 oz fresh porcini and 10 oz thinly sliced veal and cook quickly over high heat. Season well, stir in ²/3 cup light cream and bring to a simmer. Drain the pasta and toss into the veal porcini sauce. Serve sprinkled with 2 tablespoons chopped parsley and 2 tablespoons grated Parmesan cheese.

1 Chicken BLT

Serves 4

4 bacon slices
8 whole wheat bread slices
2 teaspoons whole-grain mustard
4 crisp iceburg lettuce leaves
4 tomatoes, sliced
2 store-bought, cooked chicken
   breasts, sliced
1 avocado, pitted and sliced

- Cook the bacon slices in a dry skillet until crisp.

- Meanwhile, toast the whole wheat bread on both sides, then spread 4 slices with the whole-grain mustard.

- Place a lettuce leaf on each of these slices and top with the sliced tomato. Divide the chicken among the slices of toast.

- Top with the bacon and the avocado.

- Finish with the remaining slices of toast and, using toothpicks to keep the sandwiches together, cut on the diagonal to serve.

2 Warm Chicken Salad

Cut 4 (5 oz) chicken breasts and 1 small baguette into chunks and place on a baking sheet. Sprinkle with 2 tablespoons olive oil and 2 crushed garlic cloves. Toss to coat and cook in a preheated oven, at 400°F, for 15 minutes, until the bread is crisp and the chicken is cooked through. Meanwhile, whisk together 3 tablespoons extra virgin olive oil and 1 tablespoon balsamic vinegar. In a large bowl, toss together 1 (6 oz) package spinach leaves with 12 halved cherry tomatoes and 1⅓ cups crumbled goat cheese. Arrange the cooked chicken and bread in a serving dish and toss with the spinach salad. Drizzle with the dressing to serve.

3 Stuffed Chicken Breasts

Make a slit down the side of 4 (5 oz) boneless, skinless chicken breasts to form a pocket. Stuff each pocket with 6 oz sliced Fontina or other hard cheese and a handful of basil leaves. Wrap each chicken breast with 2 slices of prosciutto. Place on a baking sheet and cook in a preheated oven, at 400°F, for 20 minutes, until cooked through. Meanwhile, heat 2 tablespoons olive oil in a skillet and toss in 8 oz baby spinach leaves and 12 cherry tomatoes. Cook briefly until the spinach starts to wilt. Serve the chicken breasts on a bed of wilted spinach.

30 Pork Cutlets with Peperonata

Serves 4

2 tablespoons olive oil

1 onion, finely diced

2 garlic cloves, crushed

2 red bell peppers, cored, seeded, and thinly sliced

1 yellow bell pepper, cored, seeded, and thinly sliced

2 tablespoons white wine

1 (14½ oz) can diced tomatoes

4 pork cutlets, about 5 oz each

1 tablespoon chopped oregano

purple baby broccoli, to serve

- Heat 1 tablespoon of the olive oil in a skillet and sauté the onion for 3–4 minutes. Add the garlic and cook for another 1 minute.

- Stir in the bell peppers and wine, bring to a simmer, cover, and cook for 10 minutes.

- Pour in the diced tomatoes and cook, uncovered, for another 10–15 minutes, until the bell peppers are soft.

- Meanwhile, pound the pork cutlets until thin, toss in the remaining olive oil and the oregano, and cook on a preheated hot ridged grill pan for 3–4 minutes on each side.

- Serve the veal on a bed of the peperonata, with steamed purple baby broccoli.

 Pork Chops with Italian Purple Baby Broccoli Cook 1½ lb purple baby broccoli in a saucepan of boiling water for 4–5 minutes. Drain. Meanwhile, dust 4 pounded pork cutlets with seasoned flour. Heat 4 tablespoons butter and 1 tablespoon olive oil in a skillet and cook the dusted pork with 2 teaspoons chopped sage leaves for 4–5 minutes, until cooked through. Heat 2 tablespoons olive oil in a skillet, add the broccoli, and cook for 1 minute. Add 2 chopped garlic cloves, ¼ teaspoon dried red pepper flakes, the juice of ½ lemon, and some pepper and cook for another 1 minute. Serve with the pork.

 Purple Baby Broccoli and Pancetta Soup Heat 2 tablespoons olive oil and sauté 8 oz diced pancetta for 1–2 minutes. Remove half from the saucepan and add 1 chopped onion and sauté for 2–3 minutes. Add 2 diced potatoes, 1 lb purple baby broccoli, and 3¾ cups vegetable stock. Bring to a boil and simmer for 8–10 minutes, until the potatoes are tender. Stir in 2 cups Gorgonzola or other blue cheese. Using a handheld blender, or in a food processor or blender, blend the soup until smooth. Stir in ²/₃ cup milk, season, and reheat gently before serving. Serve sprinkled with the remaining pancetta.

20 Lamb with Fennel and Marsala Wine

Serves 4

3 tablespoons olive oil

2 fennel bulbs, thinly sliced

2 teaspoons chopped thyme leaves

¼ cup marsala or other red wine

½ cup heavy cream

2 cups frozen peas, defrosted

1 garlic clove, finely chopped

8 lamb cutlets, about 5 oz each

- Heat 2 tablespoons of the olive oil in a skillet and sauté the fennel and thyme for 1–2 minutes, until tender.

- Stir in the marsala, heavy cream, and peas and simmer for 4–5 minutes.

- Heat the remaining oil in another skillet and sauté the garlic and lamb cutlets for 3–4 minutes on each side, until brown.

- Transfer the lamb cutlets to the vegetables and cook for another 3–4 minutes, or until cooked to your liking.

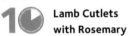 **Lamb Cutlets with Rosemary and Fennel** Steam 4 sliced fennel bulbs for 5–6 minutes until tender. Meanwhile, rub 8 lamb cutlets with a mixture of 1 tablespoon olive oil, 2 tablespoons chopped rosemary, 2 crushed garlic cloves and the grated rind of ½ lemon. Broil or pan-fry the cutlets to your liking. Remove the fennel from the steamer and place in an ovenproof dish, sprinkle with the juice of ½ lemon, 3 tablespoons fresh bread crumbs, and 3 tablespoons grated Parmesan cheese. Cook under a preheated hot broiler for 2–3 minutes, until golden. Serve with the lamb.

 Pesto-Crusted Rack of Lamb Mix together 2 tablespoons prepared pesto with ¼ cup fresh bread crumbs in a bowl. Score the fat on 2 (1 lb) racks of lamb and spread the bread crumb mixture over the fat, pressing it down. Cook in a preheated oven, at 425°F, for 14–16 minutes, or longer if you like your lamb less pink. Meanwhile, slice 3 fennel bulbs and toss in 2 tablespoons olive oil and the juice of ½ lemon. Season with pepper and cook in a hot ridged grill pan until caramelized. Serve the lamb racks with the grilled fennel and a green salad.

30 Sausage and Cranberry Bean Stew

Serves 4

2 tablespoons olive oil

4 Italian sausages, chopped

1 large onion, chopped

2 garlic cloves, chopped

1 teaspoon fennel seeds

5½ cups cherry tomatoes

2 cups beef stock

2 (15 oz) cans cranberry beans, rinsed and drained

2 cups halved, trimmed green beans

1 tablespoon chopped basil leaves

2 tablespoons grated Parmesan cheese, to serve (optional)

- Heat the olive oil in a skillet and brown the chunks of sausage for 3–4 minutes.

- Remove the sausage from the skillet and add the onion, garlic, and fennel seeds and cook for 3–4 minutes, then add the cherry tomatoes and stock.

- Bring to a simmer, return the sausages to the skillet, and add the cranberry beans.

- Cook for 10 minutes, then add the halved green beans and basil. Cook for another 5–6 minutes, until the sausages are cooked through and the beans are tender.

- Serve sprinkled with grated Parmesan, if desired.

---

10 Sausage Salad with Bean Dip

Toss together 1 cup torn romaine lettuce leaves, ⅔ cup drained and sliced roasted red peppers from a jar, 4 chopped, pitted ripe black olives, 3 sliced tomatoes, and 8 oz thickly sliced cooked Italian sausages in a salad bowl. Place 1 (15 oz) can cranberry beans, rinsed and drained, 2 crushed garlic cloves, the juice of ½ lemon, 2 tablespoons tahini, and ¼–⅓ cup extra virgin olive oil in a food processor or blender, then process until smooth, adding more oil, if needed. Serve the salad with the dip, sprinkled with 1 tablespoon extra virgin olive oil and 1 tablespoon toasted pine nuts.

20 Warm Sausage and Bean Salad

Cook 4 diagonally sliced Italian sausages under a preheated hot broiler or on a hot barbecue for 3–4 minutes, until cooked through. Steam 3½ cups green beans until tender and then refresh in cold water and drain. Toss together the sausages, beans, 1 (15 oz) can cranberry beans, drained and rinsed, 4 sliced tomatoes, and 8–10 basil leaves in a large bowl. Whisk together 3 tablespoons olive oil, 1 tablespoon sherry vinegar, 1 crushed garlic clove, ½ teaspoon whole-grain mustard, and ½ teaspoon honey in a separate bowl. Drizzle the dressing over the salad and serve with bread.

Smoked Duck Breast Salad

Serves 4

2 oranges

2 tablespoons extra virgin
olive oil

½ teaspoon Dijon mustard

3 cups watercress or arugula

a small handful of pomegranate
seeds

8 oz smoked duck breast, sliced

- Peel and segment the oranges over a bowl to catch the juice.

- Whisk the orange juice with the olive oil and Dijon mustard.

- Toss together the watercress, pomegranate seeds, and orange segments in a bowl, then divide among 4 shallow bowls.

- Top with the smoked duck breast and drizzle with the dressing to serve.

 Duck with Mushrooms and Tagliatelle Heat 2 tablespoons olive oil in a skillet and sauté 1 chopped red onion and 2 crushed garlic cloves for 1–2 minutes. Add 1 cup sliced cremini mushrooms and cook for another 4–5 minutes. Stir in ½ cup white wine, 2 teaspoons tomato paste, 10 oz smoked sliced duck breast, and ¼ cup crème fraîche or sour cream and simmer for 5–6 minutes. Meanwhile, cook 12 oz tagliatelle in a saucepan of boiling water according to the package directions, until "al dente." Drain and toss with the smoked duck sauce. Serve sprinkled with 1 tablespoon thyme leaves.

 Duck with Broccoli and Olives Score the skin of 4 (6 oz) duck breasts in a crisscross pattern, with a sharp knife. Season the skin with salt and pepper. Heat an ovenproof skillet and place the duck breasts skin side down in the skillet. Cook for 7–8 minutes, until the fat runs out and the skin is golden. Turn the breasts over and brown on the other side. Remove 1–2 tablespoons of the duck fat and place in another skillet. Transfer the duck skillet to a preheated oven, at 400°F, and cook for 8–10 minutes, depending on how rare you like your duck. Meanwhile, steam 1 large head of broccoli, cut into florets, for 3–4 minutes. Heat the duck fat in the skillet and sauté 2 diced shallots and 1 chopped red chile for 3–4 minutes and then add the steamed broccoli, tossing to coat in the spicy oil. Sprinkle in 1 cup chopped, pitted ripe black olives. Remove the duck breasts from the oven and let rest for 5 minutes before serving with the broccoli.

QuickCook

Desserts
and Cakes

Recipes listed by cooking time

30

20

10

 Coconut Kisses

Serves 4

4 tablespoons unsalted butter, melted, plus extra for greasing

3 cups shredded unsweetened dried coconut

¼ cup superfine or granulated sugar

1 egg, beaten

- Grease a baking sheet. Place the coconut, sugar, and melted butter in a bowl and mix together. Stir in the egg and mix well.

- Using your hands, take walnut-size pieces of the mixture and shape them into little pyramids. Place on the prepared baking sheet and bake in a preheated oven, at 300°F, for 15 minutes, until golden.

- Let cool on a wire rack.

10 Coconut Dessert Sprinkle

Mix together ½ tablespoon olive oil, 1 tablespoon honey, 1 tablespoon maple syrup, 1 cup rolled oats, 3 tablespoons sunflower seeds, 2 tablespoons sesame seeds, and ¼ cup slivered almonds in a bowl. Spread onto a baking sheet and cook under a preheated medium broiler for 6–7 minutes, turning often, until golden. Pour into a large bowl and stir in ⅓ cup dried cranberries and ⅓ cup unsweetened shredded dried coconut. Serve with fresh fruit and yogurt.

30 Coconut Biscotti

Mix together ½ cup superfine or granulated sugar, 1 cup all-purpose flour, 1 teaspoon baking powder, the grated rind of 1 orange, ½ cup blanched almonds, ¼ cup unsweetened shredded dried coconut, and 1 egg in a bowl to make a stiff dough. Turn out onto a floured work surface and roll into a sausage shape about 11 inches long. Place on a baking sheet and bake in a preheated oven, at 425°F, for 15 minutes. Remove from the oven, let cool for 2–3 minutes, and then gently slice into biscotti. Lay the biscotti flat on the baking sheet and bake for another 2–3 minutes to crisp. Let cool on a wire rack.

ITA-SWEE-KIM

30 Pear and Mascarpone Pancakes

Serves 4

1 cup all-purpose flour, sifted

2 eggs

1¼ cups milk

2 tablespoons butter, melted,
  plus extra for greasing

2 cups mascarpone cheese

2 tablespoons Amaretto liqueur

3 ripe pears, peeled, cored,
  and diced

¼ cup honey

- To make the pancake batter, place the flour in a large bowl and make a well in the center. Pour the eggs into the center and start to beat, bringing in the flour. Gradually add the milk, beating continuously until you have a batter the consistency of heavy cream. Beat in the melted butter.

- Grease a skillet with a little melted butter, using paper towels to remove any excess.

- Pour in a small amount of the batter, swirling it around to coat the bottom of the skillet. Cook for 1–2 minutes and then flip the pancake over to cook the other side for about 1 minute. Repeat with the remaining batter to make 8 pancakes. Stack the pancakes between sheets of wax paper, wrapped in aluminum foil to keep warm.

- Meanwhile, beat together the mascarpone and Amaretto in a bowl, then briefly fold in the diced pears and 2 tablespoons of the honey to create a rippled effect.

- Divide the mixture among the pancakes, fold each one into quarters, and place in an ovenproof dish. Drizzle with the remaining honey and heat under a preheated hot broiler for 1–2 minutes before serving.

 Pear, Blue Cheese, and Honey Crostini

Cut a thin baguette into 8 slices and toast on one side. Cut 1 pear into thin slices and place on the untoasted side of the slices. Top with ⅔ cup crumbled dolcelatte cheese and drizzle each one with ¼ teaspoon honey. Broil for 1–2 minutes, until the cheese has melted.

 Orange-Poached Pears

Combine 2 cups fresh orange juice, ⅓ cup superfine or granulated sugar, the grated rind of 1 orange, 3 cloves, and 1 cinnamon stick in a large saucepan. Add 4 peeled, cored, and quartered pears, bring to a simmer, cover, and cook for about 15 minutes, until the pears are tender. Remove the pears and boil the liquid to reduce a little. Meanwhile, beat together ¼ cup mascarpone cheese, 2 tablespoons confectioners' sugar, and the grated rind of 1 orange in a bowl. Serve the pears with a dollop of the mascarpone, drizzled with a little juice, and sprinkled with 2 tablespoons slivered almonds.

ITA-SWEE-JYE

Roasted Amaretti Peaches

Serves 4

4 peaches, halved and pitted

8 amaretti cookies

1 tablespoon honey

2 tablespoons unsalted butter, diced

For the mascarpone cream

¼ cup mascarpone cheese

2 tablespoons confectioners' sugar, sifted

2 tablespoons Amaretto liqueur

2 tablespoons toasted slivered almonds, to serve

- Place the peach halves, cut side up, in an ovenproof dish. Crumble the amaretti cookies and sprinkle them into the holes in the peaches. Drizzle with the honey.

- Dab the peaches with the butter and bake in a preheated oven, at 400°F, for 15–18 minutes, until tender.

- Meanwhile, beat together the mascarpone, confectioners' sugar, and Amaretto in a small bowl.

- Serve the peaches with a dollop of the mascarpone, sprinkled with slivered almonds.

Peachy Fruit Salad

Combine 3 pitted and chopped peaches, 2 cups hulled and sliced strawberries, 1 cup halved green seedless grapes, and 1⅔ cups raspberries in a serving bowl. Beat together the juice of 1 lime, 3 tablespoons pineapple juice, ½ teaspoon ground ginger, and 2 tablespoons shredded mint leaves in a small bowl. Pour the juices over the fruit and gently toss together. Serve with a dollop of crème fraîche or Greek yogurt.

Peach and Almond Tarts

Roll out 1 sheet ready-to-bake chilled puff pastry on a lightly floured work surface and cut it into four 4 x 5 inch rectangles. Lay them on a baking sheet. Score a border with a knife about ½ inch around the edge, then prick the bottom with a fork and brush with beaten egg. Bake in a preheated oven, at 400°F, for 10 minutes. Chop 6 oz marzipan and divide among the pastries. Slice 3 peaches and fan them out on top, followed by a sprinkling of 2 tablespoons slivered almonds. Return to the oven for another 10 minutes, until golden. Meanwhile, beat together 2 tablespoons mascarpone cheese, 2 tablespoons confectioners' sugar, and 1 tablespoon Amaretto liqueur in a bowl and serve with the tarts.

 # Sweet Ricotta and Raspberries

Serves 4

2 cups ricotta cheese
grated rind of 2 oranges
3 tablespoons honey
3 cups raspberries

- Mix together the ricotta, orange rind, and 2 tablespoons of the honey in a bowl.

- Gently stir in the raspberries.

- Divide the mixture among 4 glasses or small bowls.

- Drizzle with the remaining honey and serve immediately.

 ### Sweet Ricotta Mousse

Put 1½ cups ricotta cheese, ¾ cup mascarpone cheese, and 2 tablespoons granulated sugar in a food processor or blender and process until well mixed. Stir in the grated rind of 2 oranges and the seeds scraped from 1 vanilla bean. Whip 2 cups heavy cream with 2 tablespoons Amaretto liqueur until stiff and then gently fold into the ricotta mixture. Divide among 4 glasses and chill for 10 minutes. Serve with fresh raspberries and sprigs of mint.

 ### Baked Sweet Ricotta

Mix together 1½ cups ricotta cheese, the grated rind of 2 oranges, ⅓ cup granulated sugar, 1¼ cups almond meal (ground almonds), ¾ cup chopped candied peel, and 4 beaten eggs in a bowl. Spoon into 4 ramekin dishes and bake in a preheated oven, at 375°F, for 20–22 minutes, until risen and golden. Meanwhile, place 3 cups raspberries in a saucepan with the grated rind and juice of 1 orange and 2 tablespoons granulated sugar. Heat gently for 2–3 minutes. Serve the warm berries with the baked ricotta.

ITA-SWEE-QYL

 # Orange and Strawberry Salad

Serves 4

⅓ cup granulated sugar

½ cup water

1 tablespoon thinly sliced
  basil leaves

1 cup hulled and halved
  strawberries

4 oranges

- Put the sugar and measured water in a saucepan and bring to a boil. Simmer for 2–3 minutes and then let it cool briefly before adding the basil.

- Place the strawberries in a bowl. Peel and segment 4 oranges over the bowl to catch the juice. Add the orange segments to the strawberries.

- Pour in the syrup and serve.

 Oranges in Marsala Wine Peel 4 oranges, then slice them thinly. Place them in a shallow bowl and pour 3 tablespoons marsala wine (or Amaretto, if preferred) over the oranges. Let marinate for 10 minutes. Put ¼ cup granulated sugar and a small handful of chopped mint leaves in a mortar and crush with a pestle. Sprinkle the minted sugar and 6 crushed Amaretti cookies over the oranges and spoon into 4 serving dishes. Serve each dish with a spoonful of mascarpone cheese.

 Caramelized Oranges Peel 4 oranges, then slice them thinly. Place in a shallow serving dish and pour 1 tablespoon orange liqueur over them. Place ½ cup granulated sugar, 1 cinnamon stick, and ⅔ cup water in a saucepan. Heat, stirring, until the sugar has dissolved. Continue to simmer until the sugar starts to caramelize and turns a rich caramel color. Pour the syrup over the oranges. Decorate with ¼ cup toasted pine nuts and 1 tablespoon chopped mint leaves.

ITA-SWEE-SAO

30 Tiramisu

Serves 4

¼ cup superfine or granulated
  sugar

2 egg yolks

⅔ cup strong coffee

2 tablespoons coffee liqueur

1 cup heavy cream

1 cup mascarpone cheese

20 ladyfingers

1 teaspoon unsweeetened
  cocoa powder

- Place the sugar and egg yolks in a bowl over a saucepan of simmering water and whisk for 4–5 minutes, until light and fluffy. Let cool slightly.

- Pour the coffee into a shallow bowl and stir in the liqueur.

- Whip the cream to soft peaks.

- Stir the mascarpone into the cooled egg yolk mixture, then gently fold in the whipped cream.

- Dip half the ladyfingers into the coffee and place them in the bottom of a shallow serving dish. Spread half the cream mixture over the ladyfingers.

- Repeat with the remaining ladyfingers and cream mixture, then sift the cocoa powder over the layers.

- Chill for 10 minutes before serving.

 Very Quick Individual Tiramisu

Dip 12 ladyfingers into ½ cup strong coffee and divide them among 4 glasses or small bowls. Beat together 1 cup mascarpone cheese with 2 tablespoons coffee liqueur and spoon the mixture over the ladyfingers. Sift ½ teaspoon unsweetened cocoa powder on top and serve.

 Tiramisu Fondue

Put 1⅔ cups mascarpone cheese, 2 tablespoons strong coffee, 1 tablespoon Amaretto liqueur, 2 teaspoons cornstarch, and ⅓ cup confectioners' sugar in a bowl over a saucepan of simmering water. Gently stir as the mixture heats, gradually bringing it all together to form a smooth thick sauce. When the sauce is hot, beat 2 eggs in another bowl and pour the mascarpone mixture over them, beating continuously. Return the bowl to the heat and cook until the fondue is creamy and thick enough to dip into. Serve with chopped fruits or biscotti for dipping.

ITA-SWEE-XUA

2 Zabaglioni

Serves 4

1 vanilla bean, split lengthwise
8 egg yolks
2 tablespoons superfine or
  granulated sugar
¼ cup marsala wine
light, thin cookies, to serve

- Scrape the seeds from the split vanilla bean and place in a bowl with the egg yolks, sugar, and marsala. Whisk together with a balloon whisk.

- Place the bowl over a saucepan of simmering water, with the heat on very low, and continue to whisk for 8–10 minutes, until the mixture is very light and foamy and holds its shape.

- Spoon into 4 glasses and serve with light, thin cookies.

1 Marsala Affogato
Mix together 4 shots of espresso with 2 tablespoons marsala wine. Spoon 8 scoops of ice cream into 4 small bowls and pour the coffee mixture while still hot over the scoops. Serve sprinkled with coarsely chopped dark chocolate.

3 Plums and Panettone with Zabaglioni Halve and pit 6 plums and place in a small saucepan with the juice and grated rind of 2 oranges, ⅓ cup superfine or granulated sugar, and 1 cinnamon stick. Simmer gently for 15 minutes, until soft.

Meanwhile, make the Zabaglioni as above. Toast 4 slices of panettone on both sides and place each one on a plate. Top with the stewed plums and finally spoon over the zabaglioni. Serve immediately.

ITA-SWEE-TUP

30 Honeyed Figs

Serves 4

12 figs
2 tablespoons unsalted butter
¼ cup honey
¼ teaspoon ground cinnamon

To serve (optional)

¼ cup mascarpone cheese
½ cup toasted slivered almonds

- Cut a cross in the top of each fig, not quite cutting all the way through. Place in an ovenproof dish.

- Melt together the butter, honey, and cinnamon in a saucepan and pour the mixture over the figs.

- Bake in a preheated oven, at 400°F, for 20 minutes.

- Serve the figs with a dollop of mascarpone and sprinkled with slivered almonds, if liked.

 Figs with Honey and Cheese

Slice a ciabatta loaf into 4 by first cutting in half vertically and then again horizontally. Lightly toast the bread on both sides. Divide 2 cups Gorgonzola cheese between the 4 slices. Top each one with 1 sliced fig and then drizzle with 1 tablespoon honey.

 Fig Scones

Mix together 4 cups all-purpose flour, ½ cup superfine or granulated sugar, and ¼ cup baking powder in a bowl. Add 6 tablespoons unsalted butter and rub in with your fingertips until the mixture ressembles bread crumbs. Gently stir in 2 beaten eggs, 1 cup milk, and ½ cup chopped dried figs, until you have a soft dough. Turn out onto a lightly floured work surface and roll or press out to a thickness of about 1½ inches. Cut out 6–8 scones using a 1½–2 inch pastry cutter and place on a baking sheet. Bake in a preheated oven, at 400°F, for 15 minutes, until golden and risen. Let cool on a wire rack.

ITA-SWEE-GAU

30 Pear Strudel

Serves 4–6

3 pears, peeled, cored, and diced
½ cup raisins
¼ cup frozen cranberries
⅔ cup superfine or granulated
  sugar
grated rind of 1 orange
8 sheets of phyllo pastry
4 tablespoons unsalted butter,
  melted
3 tablespoons almond meal
  (ground almonds)
plain yogurt, to serve

- Place the diced pears, raisins, and cranberries in a small saucepan with the sugar and orange rind and cook over low heat for 2–3 minutes, until the pears start to soften.

- Place 1 sheet of phyllo on the work surface and brush with melted butter. Lay another sheet on top and brush with more butter. Repeat with the remaining sheets of phyllo.

- Sprinkle the buttered pastry sheets with the almond meal.

- Spoon the pear and raisin mixture down the center of the pastry and roll into a sausage shape, folding in the ends to enclose the fruit.

- Place on a baking sheet and brush with the remaining melted butter.

- Bake in a preheated oven, at 375°F, for 20–25 minutes, until golden.

- Cut into slices and serve with yogurt.

 Poached Pears with Blackberries

Thinly slice 4 pears and poach them in 1¾ cups sweet red wine for 8 minutes. At the end of the cooking time, gently stir in 3 tablespoons blackberries. Serve with vanilla ice cream.

 Ricotta-Filled Pears

Beat ½ cup ricotta cheese with 1 tablespoon confectioners' sugar and 1 tablespoon unsweetened cocoa powder in a bowl. Stir in 2 oz chopped semisweet dark chocolate and the grated rind of 1 orange. Peel 2 ripe pears, cut in half lengthwise, and remove the cores. Brush the pears with 2 tablespoons orange juice, then spoon in the ricotta filling. Serve sprinkled with mint leaves.

Watermelon and Pineapple with Sambuca

Serves 4

½ small watermelon

1 small pineapple

4 shots of Sambuca

2 tablespoons toasted slivered almonds

4 scoops of vanilla ice cream, to serve

- Peel the watermelon and pineapple and cut into ½ inch thick slices.

- Stack the slices on top of each other on 4 serving plates, alternating the fruits.

- Pour 1 shot of the Sambuca over each stack, sprinkle with the slivered almonds, and serve with a scoop of vanilla ice cream.

Watermelon, Pineapple, and

Peaches Melt 1½ tablespoons butter in a small skillet and toast 2 tablespoons slivered almonds, until golden. Let cool. Thinly slice 4 peaches and toss together with ½ small peeled and cubed watermelon and ½ small peeled and chopped pineapple in a bowl. Mix together 2 tablespoons honey, ¼ teaspoon ground cinnamon, and ⅓ cup plain yogurt in another bowl. Divide the fruit among 4 small bowls and pour the yogurt dressing over the fruit. Sprinkle with the toasted almonds to serve.

Pineapple Fritters

Sift 1⅔ cups all-purpose flour into a bowl and then beat in ½ cup warm water, ½ cup beer, ½ tablespoon vegetable oil, and ½ tablespoon marsala wine to make a batter. Cut 1 large cored and peeled pineapple into thick slices. Pour sunflower oil into a deep-fat fryer or large saucepan and heat to 350–375°F, or until a cube of bread dropped into the oil browns in 30 seconds. Beat 2 egg whites into the batter and then dip in the pineapple slices, shaking off any excess. Working in batches, if necessary, carefully drop into the hot oil. Deep-fry for 3–4 minutes, until golden all over. Remove with a slotted spoon and drain on paper towels. Serve sprinkled with torn mint leaves and dusted with sugar.

20 Amaretti Cookies

Serves 8

2 extra-large egg whites
2 cups almond meal
(ground almonds)
1 cup superfine or granulated
sugar
3 teaspoons Amaretto liqueur

- Line a baking sheet with parchment paper. Place the egg whites in a clean, grease-free bowl and beat with a handheld electric mixer until soft peaks form.

- Gently fold in the almond meal, sugar, and Amaretto.

- Place teaspoons of the dough at least 1 inch apart on the prepared baking sheet.

- Bake in a preheated oven, at 325°F, for 15 minutes, until golden.

- Let cool on a wire rack.

1 Raspberries with Almond Crisp

Place 3¼ cups raspberries in an ovenproof dish. Mix together 3½ tablespoons melted butter, 2 tablespoons superfine or granulated sugar, and 1¼ cups almond meal (ground almonds) in a bowl. Coarsely spread the almond mixture over the fruit and cook under a preheated medium-hot broiler for 5–6 minutes, until golden. Serve with light cream.

3 Almond Shortbread

Cream together 1 stick softened unsalted butter and ¼ cup superfine or granulated sugar until light and fluffy. Stir in ¾ cup plus 1 tablespoon all-purpose flour, 1¼ teaspoons baking powder, ¼ cup almond meal (ground) almonds, and a few drops of Amaretto liqueur. Place 8–10 walnut-size balls of the dough at least 1 inch apart on a greased baking sheet. Press each one down lightly with a fork and then bake in a preheated oven, at 350°F, for 15 minutes, until golden. Let cool on a wire rack.

30 Sweet Berry Pizzas

Serves 4

3⅔ cups white bread flour, plus extra for dusting

¼ cup superfine or granulated sugar

2¼ teaspoons active dry yeast

a pinch of salt

1 tablespoon olive oil

1¼ cups warm water

1¼ cups cream cheese

3 extra-large egg yolks

2–3 drops of vanilla extract

3½–4 cups fresh mixed berries, such as raspberries, blueberries, and halved or quartered strawberries

¾ cup firmly packed light brown sugar

¼ cup all-purpose flour

4 tablespoons unsalted butter, melted

- To make the dough, place the bread flour, 2 tablespoons of the sugar, the yeast, and salt in a large bowl and mix together. Make a well in the center. Stir in the olive oil and most of the measured water. Mix together with your hand, gradually adding more water, if necessary, until you have a soft but not sticky dough.

- Turn out the dough onto a floured work surface and knead for 5–10 minutes, until the dough is smooth and elastic.

- Divide the dough into 4 pieces and roll out to 6 inch circles, then place on 2 large baking sheets.

- Mix together the cream cheese, egg yolks, vanilla extract, and remaining superfine sugar and spread over the pizza crusts. Top with the berries.

- Mix together the brown sugar, all-purpose flour, and melted butter in a bowl and sprinkle over the berries.

- Bake in a preheated oven, at 425°F, for 12–15 minutes, until golden.

 Sweet Pita Breads

Toast 4 pita breads on both sides. Mix together 1 cup cream cheese with 2 tablespoons light brown sugar in a bowl and spread over the pita breads. Sprinkle each one with ½ cup raspberries and drizzle with 2 teaspoons honey. Cook under a preheated hot broiler for 2–3 minutes and serve sprinkled with 1 teaspoon toasted sesame seeds.

 Quick Sweet Calzones

Mix together 1 cup cream cheese, 1 egg yolk, and 2 tablespoons superfine or granulated sugar in a bowl. Lay 4 flour tortillas on the work surface and spread half of each one with the cream cheese mixture, leaving a 1 inch clean edge. Add 1½ cups hulled and sliced strawberries and a small handful of blueberries.

Brush beaten egg around the clean edges of each tortilla and then fold over the other halves to make semicircles. Press down the edges to seal. Heat 2 tablespoons butter and 1 tablespoon olive oil in a skillet and sauté the tortillas for 3–4 minutes on each side, until golden.

ITA-SWEE-POR

 # Apple and Parmesan Tarts

Serves 4

flour, for dusting

1 sheet store-bought chilled puff pastry

2 teaspoons light brown sugar

2 tart apples, peeled, cored, and sliced

2 teaspoons honey

½ cup grated Parmesan cheese

For the mascarpone cream (optional)

¼ cup mascarpone cheese

grated rind and juice of ½ lemon

1 teaspoon dark brown sugar

- Line a baking sheet with parchment paper. Roll the pastry out on a lightly floured work surface and cut out four 4 x 5 inch rectangles. Place them on the baking sheet and sprinkle with the light brown sugar.

- Arrange the apple slices in a line on each rectangle of pastry. Drizzle each one with the honey and then sprinkle with the grated Parmesan.

- Bake in a preheated oven, at 400°F, for 12–14 minutes, until golden.

- Meanwhile, to make the mascarpone cream, if using, beat together the mascarpone, lemon rind and juice, and brown sugar in a bowl.

- Serve each tart with a dollop of mascarpone cream, if liked.

 Toffee Apples with Rice Pudding

Melt 1 stick butter and 3 tablespoons honey in a saucepan. Add 4 peeled, cored, and sliced apples and warm for 3–4 minutes in the syrup. Serve the toffee apples spooned over 4 single-serving, store-bought rice pudding cups, heated according to the package directions.

 Apple Fritters

Sift together 1¼ cups all-purpose flour, 1¾ teaspoons baking powder, and 1 teaspoon ground cinnamon in a bowl. Stir in ¼ cup granulated sugar. Whisk in 1 cup apple juice to make a batter slightly thicker than the consistency of heavy cream. Pour sunflower oil into a deep-fat fryer or large saucepan and heat to 350–375°F, or until a cube of bread dropped into the oil browns in 30 seconds. Peel and core 4 apples, remove the tops and bottoms, and then slice into ½ inch thick rings. Dip the apple slices into the batter and then, working in batches, carefully drop into the hot oil. Deep-fry for 1–2 minutes, until golden. Remove with a slotted spoon and drain on paper towels. Dust with confectioners' sugar and serve with mascarpone.

ITA-SWEE-WYT

 # Creamy Peach and Banana Smoothies

Serves 4

1 large banana

3 peaches, peeled, halved, and pitted

2 pieces of preserved ginger

1 cup plain yogurt

⅔ cup milk, plus extra if needed

- Place the banana, peaches, preserved ginger, yogurt, and milk in a food processor or blender and blend until smooth, adding more milk, if necessary.

- Pour into 4 glasses and serve immediately.

 ### Peaches with Spiced Ricotta

Toast 2 tablespoons almond meal (ground almonds) in a dry-skillet for 2–3 minutes and then stir them into 1 cup ricotta cheese with ¼ teaspoon ground cinnamon, the grated rind of ½ orange, and 2 diced pieces of preserved ginger. Halve and pit 4 peaches, then place in an ovenproof dish. Spoon the filling into each one and cook under a preheated hot broiler for 4–5 minutes.

 ### Raisin-Stuffed Peaches

Place ⅔ cup raisins in a bowl and pour ½ cup rum over them. Let stand for 10 minutes. Place 1 halved and pitted peach in a food processor or blender and process to a pulp. Stir in 1 tablespoon superfine or granulated sugar and the marinated raisins. Place another 4 halved and pitted peaches in an ovenproof dish and spoon the peach pulp and raisins into the center of each one. Pour ½ cup white wine around the peaches. Bake in a preheated oven, at 400°F, for 15 minutes, sprinkling with 2 tablespoons slivered almonds for the last minute of cooking. Serve with vanilla ice cream or crème fraîche.

30 Biscotti

Serves 4

½ cup superfine or granulated
  sugar
1 cup all-purpose flour, plus extra
  for dusting
1 teaspoon baking powder
grated rind of 1 lemon
½ cup blanched almonds
2 tablespoons dried cranberries
1 egg, beaten

- Place all of the ingredients in a bowl and, using your hands, bring them together to make a stiff dough.

- Turn out onto a floured work surface and roll into a sausage shape about 11 inches long. Place on a baking sheet and bake in a preheated oven, at 425°F, for 15 minutes.

- Remove from the oven, let cool for 2–3 minutes, and then gently slice into biscotti.

- Lay the biscotti flat on the baking sheet, return to the oven, and cook for another 2–3 minutes to crisp.

- Let cool on a wire rack.

---

1 Creamy Peach, Cranberry, and Raspberry Biscotti Desserts

Process 10 store-bought biscotti in a food processor or a blender, then mix with 3½ tablespoons melted butter. Press the mixture into the bottom of 4 ramekin dishes. Divide 2 halved, pitted, and chopped peaches, ⅓ cup dried cranberries, and 1 cup raspberries among the dishes. Spoon 2 tablespoons plain yogurt into each ramekin and sprinkle with 2 teaspoons dark brown sugar. Chill for 2 minutes before serving.

2 Cranberry and Almond Scones

Sift together 1¾ cups all-purpose flour, 2¾ teaspoons baking powder, and a pinch of salt in a large bowl. Add 6 tablespoons unsalted butter and rub in with your fingertips until the mixture resembles bread crumbs. Stir in ¼ cup superfine or granulated sugar, 3 tablespoons dried cranberries, and ¼ cup slivered almonds. Beat together 1 egg and 2 tablespoons buttermilk and mix into the flour mixture until you have a soft dough. Turn out onto a lightly floured work surface and roll or press out to a thickness of 1 inch. Cut out 10 scones using a 2 inch pastry cutter and place on a baking sheet. Bake in a preheated oven, at 425°F, for 10–12 minutes, until golden and risen. Let cool on a wire rack.

30 Honeyed Fig Whip

Serves 4

5 figs (8 oz)
grated rind of 1 orange
3 tablespoons fresh orange juice
2 tablespoons honey
1 cup plain or Greek yogurt

To serve

1 tablespoon toasted slivered
  almonds
amaretti cookies

- Place the figs, orange rind and juice, and honey in a small saucepan and simmer for 12–15 minutes, until soft and creamy. Let cool slightly.

- Place the figs in a food processor or blender and blend until smooth. Stir in the yogurt, not mixing too thoroughly, to create a marbled effect.

- Spoon into 4 small bowls or glasses and serve sprinkled with slivered almonds, along with amaretti cookies for dipping.

1 Fruit Kebabs

Thread 1½ cups hulled and halved strawberries, 3 pitted peaches, cut into wedges, and 4 quartered figs onto wooden kebab skewers. Melt 2 oz semisweet dark chocolate with 2 tablespoons heavy cream and 1 teaspoon honey in a saucepan, then drizzle the sauce over the kebabs. Serve sprinkled with 2 tablespoons toasted slivered almonds.

2 Strawberry and Fig Bruschetta

Toast 8 slices of ciabatta on both sides. Stir ¼ cup honey, 2 teaspoons grated lemon rind, and 2 teaspoons lemon juice in a small saucepan and cook until the honey has melted a little. Stir in 1 cup hulled and halved strawberries and 3 quartered figs, cook for 1 minute, then remove from the heat. Spoon ½ tablespoon mascarpone cheese onto each piece of toast and spoon the strawberries and figs on top. Serve immediately.

30 Ricotta Pancakes with Oranges and Figs

Serves 4

½ cup milk
1 cup ricotta cheese
⅔ cup all-purpose flour
½ teaspoon baking powder
2 eggs, separated
1 tablespoon granulated sugar
2 tablespoons butter
2 oranges
2 teaspoons honey
3 figs, quartered

- Place the milk, ricotta, flour, baking powder, egg yolks, and sugar in a food processor or blender and process until smooth.

- Beat the egg whites in a bowl with a handheld electric mixer until soft peaks form, then fold this into the processed batter.

- Melt the butter in a nonstick skillet, drop spoonfuls of the batter into the skillet, and cook for 2–3 minutes on each side, until golden. Cook in batches, keeping the pancakes warm, until all the batter is used.

- Peel and segment the oranges over a bowl to catch the juice. Place the juice and honey in a saucepan and warm through.

- Serve 3 pancakes per person on a plate with orange segments, pieces of fig, and the juice and honey poured over the top.

---

1 Souffléd Orange Omelet

Beat 2 egg whites in a bowl with a handheld electric mixer until soft peaks form. In a separate bowl, beat 2 egg yolks with 1½ tablespoons granulated sugar. Fold the egg whites into the egg yolks. Melt ½ tablespoon butter in a flameproof omelet pan and pour in the eggs. Let cook over low heat for 2–3 minutes, then drop in the segments of 1 orange. Sift with 1 teaspoon confectioners' sugar and cook under a preheated hot broiler for 1–2 minutes, until slightly golden.

2 Caramelized Oranges with

Sweet Ricotta Pare the rind from 2 oranges and cut into fine threads. Peel and segment 6 large oranges, reserving the juice, placing them both on a heatproof serving platter. Slowly cook 1¼ cups superfine or granulated sugar in a saucepan over medium heat, until it starts to melt. When the sugar starts to caramelize, pour in 1 cup hot water and reduce the heat to low. Add the orange rind and simmer for 5 minutes. Pour the hot syrup over the orange segments. Mix together 1½ cups ricotta with 1 tablespoon honey in a bowl. Serve the oranges with a dollop of the ricotta cheese and sprinkled with 2 tablespoons toasted pine nuts.

Amaretto Apricot Dessert

Serves 4

1 (15 oz) can apricots in syrup
2 tablespoons Amaretto liqueur
4 scoops of vanilla ice cream
8 Amaretti cookies, crushed

- Drain the syrup from the apricots into a saucepan and simmer to reduce a little, then stir in the Amaretto.

- Divide the apricots among 4 bowls and pour the warm syrup over the fruit.

- Add a scoop of vanilla ice cream to each dish and serve sprinkled with the crushed amaretti cookies.

 Vanilla-Roasted Apricots and Figs with Spiced Mascarpone

Cut a cross in the top of 8 figs, making sure not to cut all the way through. Place them in a roasting pan with 6 halved and pitted apricots. Scrape the seeds from 1 split vanilla bean, then cut the bean into 3 pieces. Put both in a mortar and pestle with ¼ cup superfine or granulated sugar and grind together until well mixed. Sprinkle the sugar over the fruit and roast in a preheated oven, at 400°F, for 12–15 minutes, until starting to caramelize. Meanwhile, blend 3 pieces of preserved ginger and 4 teaspoons ginger syrup in a small blender, then beat into 1 cup mascarpone cheese. Serve the fruits topped with a dollop of the mascarpone and a sprinkling of ground nutmeg.

 Apricot Pancakes with Orange Mascarpone

Sift 1¼ cups all-purpose flour, 2 teaspoons baking powder, and a pinch of baking soda into a bowl. Stir in 2 tablespoons superfine or granulated sugar. Beat together 1 egg and ⅔ cup milk in a separate bowl, then beat into the flour until smooth. Stir in ⅓ cup chopped dried apricots. Grate the rind of 1 orange, then segment over a bowl to catch the juice. Stir the rind, juice, and segments into 1 cup mascarpone cheese with 1 tablespoon orange liqueur. Heat 1 teaspoon olive oil in a skillet and drop in ¼ cup of batter. Cook for 1 minute, then flip over and cook for another minute. Repeat with the rest of the batter. Serve 3–4 warm pancakes per person with a large dollop of the mascarpone.

ITA-SWEE-ZAN

30 Candied Peel Cassata

Serves 4

9½ oz store-bought pound cake

1¼ cups ricotta cheese

⅓ cup chopped candied peel

1 oz semisweet dark chocolate, chopped

2 tablespoons superfine or granulated sugar

2 tablespoons Amaretto liqueur

- Line an 8½ x 4½ x 2½ inch loaf pan with plastic wrap, leaving enough hanging over the sides to be able to fold across the top.

- Slice the pound cake into 3 slices horizontally.

- Mix together the ricotta, candied peel, chocolate, and sugar in a bowl.

- Place 1 slice of cake in the bottom of the loaf pan. Spoon half the ricotta mixture on top and spread to cover the cake.

- Repeat with a second slice of cake and the remaining ricotta.

- Cover with the remaining slice of cake and sprinkle with the Amaretto.

- Pull the plastic wrap over the top to seal, press down gently, and then place in the freezer for 20 minutes to set.

---

10 Pears with Candied Peel Ricotta

Peel, core, and slice 4 pears and place in 4 small bowls. Stir 1 tablespoon Amaretto liqueur and 2 tablespoons chopped candied peel into ⅔ cup ricotta cheese. Divide among the 4 bowls and drizzle 1 teaspoon honey over each one. Serve immediately.

20 Candied Peel and Chocolate Scones

Sift 1¾ cups all-purpose flour and 2¾ teaspoons baking powder into a bowl. Add ¾ stick butter and rub in with your fingertips until the mixture resembles bread crumbs. Stir in ¼ cup sugar, 1 tablespoon chopped dark chocolate, and ½ tablespoon chopped candied peel. Beat together 1 egg and 2 tablespoons buttermilk and mix into the flour mixture until you have a soft dough. Turn out onto a floured work surface and press or roll out to a thickness of 1 inch. Cut out 10 scones using a 2 inch pastry cutter and place on a baking sheet. Bake in a preheated oven, at 425°F, for 10–12 minutes, until risen.

30 Chocolate Amaretti Lava Cakes

Serves 4

1 stick unsalted butter, plus extra, melted, for greasing

1 teaspoon unsweetened cocoa powder, sifted

4 oz dark chocolate, chopped

3 extra-large eggs

⅔ cup superfine or granulated sugar

¼ cup all-purpose flour

10 amaretti cookies, crumbled

- Brush 4 large ramekin dishes with the melted butter and shake in the cocoa powder to coat.

- Melt the chocolate and butter in a bowl over a saucepan of simmering water.

- Meanwhile, beat together the eggs and sugar until light and fluffy.

- Stir the chocolate, flour, and crumbled amaretti cookies into the egg mixture.

- Divide among the prepared ramekin dishes and bake in the preheated oven, at 375°F, for 12–15 minutes, until they have risen.

1 Chocolate and Amaretto Dessert

Melt 2¼ oz dark chocolate, 2½ tablespoons unsalted butter, and 2 tablespoons light corn syrup in a small saucepan, stirring occasionally, until you have a smooth chocolate sauce. Place a few amaretti cookies into 4 ramekin dishes, sprinkle ½ teaspoon Amaretto liqueur over each, then pour the chocolate sauce over the top. Serve with crème fraîche, sprinkled with unsweetened cocoa powder.

2 Quick Chocolate Mousse

Heat 1¼ cups heavy cream in a small saucepan until boiling. Stir in 8 oz chopped dark chocolate and stir until melted. Pour into a bowl and place this bowl in another bowl of ice to rapidly cool. Pour in 1¼ cups heavy cream, 1–2 tablespoons Amaretto liqueur, and 10–12 crumbled amaretti cookies. Beat until soft peaks form. Spoon into glasses or small bowls and serve.

Index

Page references in *italics* indicate
photographs

Acknowledgments

Recipes by: **Joy Skipper**
Executive Editor: **Eleanor Maxfield**
Senior Editor: **Leanne Bryan**
Copy Editor: **Abi Waters**
Art Direction: **Tracy Killick Art Direction and Design**
Original Design Concept: **www.gradedesign.com**
Designer: **Sally Bond for Tracy Killick Art Direction and Design**
Photographer: **Lis Parsons**
Home Economist: **Joy Skipper**
Prop Stylist: **Liz Hippisley**
Production Controller: **Davide Pontiroli**